THE
CUXHAVEN
RAID

HMS *Engadine* as she appeared after 1915 when her canvas aircraft screens were replaced with a large steel hangar. Note the wrecked aircraft on deck. She carried three Folders for embarkation in the Cuxhaven Raid. *Fleet Air Arm Museum*

THE
CUXHAVEN
RAID

The World's First Carrier Air Strike

R D Layman

CONWAY
MARITIME PRESS

© R D Layman 1985

First published in Great Britain by
Conway Maritime Press Ltd, 24 Bride Lane,
Fleet Street, London EC4Y 8DR

ISBN 0 85177 327 3

Designed by Dave Mills

Typesetting and page make-up by Swanston Graphics, Derby

Printed and bound in Great Britain by Butler and Tanner,
Frome

Contents

Sources and Acknowledgements

My archival source for the British side of the Cuxhaven Raid is Air 1/2099, 'Seaplane Operations Against Cuxhaven Carried Out on 25th December 1914', Public Record Office, a document described more fully in the introduction to notes and references for chapter 4. Quotations from this document are by permission of the Controller of Her Majesty's Stationery Office.

For the German side, I relied largely on volume 3 of Otto Groos' *Der Krieg in der Nordsee*, part of the overall history *Der Krieg zur See, 1914-1918*, published between 1920 and 1966.

My greatest debt of gratitude is to Theresa FitzGerald for research in the Public Record Office without which this study could not have been attempted or completed. Others in the United Kingdom to whom I am grateful are J M Bruce, keeper of aircraft and research studies, Royal Air Force Museum, for advising on and encouraging the project; R H Nailer, for points of information on British seaplane carriers; the late Group Captain Reginald John Bone (RAF, retired) for sharing memories of his days as a Royal Naval Air Service pilot attached to HMS *Empress*; Peter K Simpson, for securing information from Group Captain Bone, and J D Brown, head of the Naval Historical Branch, for assistance in identification of British destroyers involved in the Cuxhaven Raid.

To the West German naval historian, Fregattenkapitän a D Paul Schmalenbach, I am grateful for supplementary information and helpful comment. In the United States, I owe thanks to William P Avery, Rosalie Stemer, Judith Stone and the Hoover Institution on War, Revolution and Peace for help with bibliographic research; August G Blume, for providing a very useful unpublished manuscript; Dr Douglas H Robinson, author of the definitive history of the German naval airship, for encouraging comment and supplementary information; Adele B Hermann, for German translation, and Martha Griffin, for her always immaculate typing.

Outstanding assistance in obtaining photographs was given by: in the United States, the National Archives, US Naval Photographic Center and Dr Douglas H Robinson; in Canada by Kenneth Macpherson; in the United Kingdom by the Imperial War Museum, Dr Arthur Hewlett (son of Francis E T Hewlett), Michael B Goodall, J Syred, and the Fleet Air Arm Museum, its curator, Graham Mottram, and L F Lovell of the research department, and to G S Leslie.

As always, my greatest source of support, sympathy and inspiration was my wife, Marget Murray Layman, to whom I owe boundless and eternal gratitude.

Note on Time and Terminology

All times given in this narrative are Greenwich Mean Time, one hour earlier then Central European Standard Time. The latter is the time zone in which most of the action of the Cuxhaven Raid occurred, and its times are used in German accounts and some English language works based on German sources.

Some contemporary usages of 1914 have been altered. The type of vessel called 'torpedo boat destroyer' by the British and 'torpedo boat' by the Germans is called 'destroyer'. 'Maxim', a word in both British and German usage, is changed to 'machine gun'. In quotations from translated German material, 'U-Boot', especially in reference to British undersea craft, is rendered as 'submarine'.

Ranks of all persons mentioned are those held in December, 1914. Some later ranks are given parenthetically or in footnotes.

German naval ranks are given in the original, since some have no exact English equivalent. In general, Grossadmiral corresponds to the British admiral of the fleet and the American admiral of the navy, Fregattenkapitän to captain, Korvettenkapitän to commander, Kapitänleutnant to lieutenant commander, Oberleutnant zur See to lieutenant, and Leutnant zur See to the British sub-lieutenant and the American lieutenant junior grade.

Geographical spellings are those current in 1914.

The loss was not very great, but the daring of the attempt was very great indeed

Philip II

I look upon the events ... as a visible proof of the probable line in the development of the principles of naval strategy

Cecil J L'Estrange Malone

Introduction

The Cuxhaven Raid is the name that came to be given to an attempt by the British navy on Christmas Day 1914 to attack a German airship base by means of seaplanes carried by surface vessels. As such, it was a product of the circumstances, strategies and technologies of early World War I. But it was a unique event in the history of warfare. It was the first attempt to exert sea power upon land by means of the air – 'projection', in the jargon of today's strategists – and it resulted in the first sea battle of a type that would become common in World War II, an engagement in which aircraft alone were the primary striking arms of both sides.* It was the birth of what would become the 'carrier task force' concept, being the first time that a multiple number of aircraft operated from a multiple number of surface ships.

The Cuxhaven Raid thereby became one of those events like the Armada and Hampton Roads that mark a dividing line between epochs of naval warfare even though they are not recognized as such at the time. The historiography of the Cuxhaven Raid reveals how little the revolution in sea combat it portended was realized between 1914 and 1940. It occupies the few pages that a minor operation could be expected to command in the British official air and naval histories of World War I. More attention was given to it in the German official naval history, but only because that massive work devoted more space to everything. There were few other commentaries; it was not mentioned at all in the books by the two great North Sea antagonists, Admirals Jellicoe and Scheer.

Only after World War II were historians and strategists able to look back beyond Midway and Coral Sea, Pearl Harbor and Taranto, and find in the Cuxhaven Raid the prototype operation of the new era of naval warfare. This historical status has been

---

* It was not, strictly speaking, history's first aero-naval battle. That event occurred on 27 November 1914 when Japanese naval seaplanes attacked German and Austro-Hungarian warships in Kiaochow Bay at Tsingtao.

recognized in many books written since, but the episode itself has never been given more than a cursory examination of a few paragraphs.*

This book is an attempt to describe the operation in more detail, examining its preliminaries, planning, results, aftermath, and immediate influence, as well as its execution. For the Cuxhaven Raid was not only the pioneer attempt to merge aero- and naval technologies, but an event of intrinsic importance to the naval operations of World War I and an illustration of the extension of an old principle of British naval strategy in a new context.

There are gaps in the story – contradictions that cannot be reconciled and mysteries that the passage of decades and destruction of records make impossible to solve. But the main outline is clear, and what emerges is a view of the genesis of a new era in human conflict at sea.

* After this book was written but before its publication a fairly extended description of the raid appeared in James Goldrick's *The King's Ships Were at Sea: The War in the North Sea, August 1914 – February 1915* (Naval Institute Press, Annapolis, 1984). The treatment is undetailed in regard to aerial aspects, however, and in some respects its accuracy is open to question.

CHAPTER 1

Monsters of the Purple Twilight

The reason for the Cuxhaven Raid resided in the apprehension created in British minds by the rigid airship – specifically, by the craft named after its creator, the persevering German genius Count Ferdinand Adolf August Heinrich von Zeppelin. As World War I began this craft was not yet the important and inhibitive influence on the North Sea naval conflict that it became when, thanks to its long range and endurance and in the absence of a counterpart in the Royal Navy, it was to give Germany's High Seas Fleet a greatly superior aerial scouting capability. Instead, it was seen through British eyes as playing a much deadlier role – that of a bomb-laden raider able to cast widespread havoc over the British Isles.

The start of the chain of events leading to this apprehension can be traced to an exact date just over half a century earlier, when Zeppelin, then a 25-year-old Oberleutant in the army of the kingdom of Württenberg, went aloft in a balloon at St Paul, Minnesota. Zeppelin had been in the United States since May 1863, as a sanctioned military observer of the American Civil War. After having seen a fair amount of action, he took leave of his official duties to make an exploratory journey to the still somewhat exotic wilds of the northern Midwest and there, in St Paul, encountered a balloonist named John Steiner. On 19 August 1863, Steiner gave the young officer a tethered ascent.

Steiner had been a member of the recently disbanded Union Army balloon corps, and in March the previous year had been responsible for a landmark event, although one quickly relegated to obscurity: from a flat-boat in the Mississippi River he had taken aloft officers of a mortar boat flotilla to direct gunfire against a Confederate island stronghold.[1] It was the first use of an aerial vehicle to guide the offensive power of naval surface craft, a technique that would not be repeated in combat until 1911.

Steiner's native language was German; his English, whether

spoken or written, was ludicrously fractured to the point of unintelligibility. It must therefore have been a pleasure for him to have encountered someone with whom he could converse in his native tongue. He told Zeppelin of a new kind of balloon he hoped to build, not conventionally spherical, but 'lang und mager' (long and slender) with a rudder for steering.

This incident was the inspiration for the work that ultimately resulted in the creation of Zeppelin's rigid airship.[2] More than three decades, however, were to elapse before that craft became a reality. Although Zeppelin put his first thoughts about it on paper in 1874, his real work did not start until 1892. The previous year his championship of his native Württenberg against the increasing Prussian control of the Imperial German Army resulted in his being pressured out of service at the age of 52 with the rank of lieutenant-general.

The concept of the rigid airship – a strong structural skeleton that maintained the shape of the envelope and contained within it individual bags or balloonets of lifting gas – was not totally original with Zeppelin, but he was the first to develop it successfully. His first airship flew in June 1900, but was no more than a prototype that was discarded the next year after demonstrating some of the problems yet to be overcome, and exhausting the finances of the joint stock company that had been formed to build it. The second flew in early 1906, and its destruction by a storm after engine failure on its second flight was the first of a series of heart-breaking and bankrupting setbacks. Throwing the remains of his family fortune into the effort, Zeppelin produced a third ship. This proved the most successful yet, but was unable to meet the performance standards that the German army, now taking interest in the airship, laid down as prerequisites for purchase of one. The Count determinedly started on a fourth ship, completing it in June 1908. It met a fate similar to the second, destruction by storm and fire after engine failure.

With this disaster, the story might have ended and the reason for the Cuxhaven Raid never have come into existence. But Zeppelin's dogged perseverance in the face of repeated setbacks had made him a national hero, a symbol of Teutonic scientific progress. In a great groundswell of sympathy and admiration, individuals began to send him monetary contributions for the continuation of his work. The idea caught on, and soon the number of donors grew to thousands; the gifts eventually totalled nearly $1.5 million. The Count sagely set up a foundation to manage this windfall (the Zeppelin Foundation for the Promotion of Aerial Navigation), which financed establishment of the

Zeppelin Airship Company (Luftschiffbau Zeppelin). This firm would produce the majority of rigid airships used by Germany in World War I.

He also founded an aerial joy-riding firm, the German Airship Transportation Company (quickly known as DELAG, a contraction of Deutsche Luftschiffahrt A G). Often called the world's first airline, this company did not run scheduled flights but simply took small groups of passengers up for leisurely excursions over the countryside in a more sophisticated and more reliable form of free ballooning, a sport popular among a small fringe of the monied classes of Edwardian–Wilhelmine Europe.

These developments occurred during 1909, and although Zeppelin was to suffer further setbacks and losses and was again to skirt financial ruination, that year may be said to have seen the establishment of his ships as viable vehicles. It also saw the purchase of two Zeppelins by the army, thus introducing the rigid airship into German military aeronautics.[3]

Another development in 1909 was the arrival of a competitor to Zeppelin, the Luftschiffbau Schütte-Lanz, whose first ship flew in 1911. This and succeeding Schütte-Lanz ships differed from Zeppelins in having structures made of laminated plywood instead of aluminium alloy but also incorporated aerodynamic and other technical features superior to the Count's craft. Many of these patented innovations were made available to the Zeppelin firm by the German government after the start of World War I. But the contributions of Schütte-Lanz designs to the advancement of rigid airship technology were known to few outside German technical circles, and by 1914 the entire mystique of the airship was summed up in the magic and menacing word 'Zeppelin'.

The aura of sinister mystery surrounding the Zeppelin during the last prewar years in Europe was generated by a number of factors. Perhaps the greatest was the most obvious – the very appearance of the craft. The rigid airship, probably the most impressive object man has ever placed in the sky, was a majestic, awe-inspiring sight, truly gigantic. Even the early Zeppelins were huge things, rivalling the mightiest battleships and ocean liners in length. The rigid's stately, serene path through the blue produced a sensation of overwhelming power. The typical aeroplane of the period seemed as insubstantial and insignificant as an insect in comparison.

The superiority of the airship to the aeroplane was not merely a matter of appearance. It *was* superior in the three catagories of performance that seemed most important to a flying craft in peace or war: it could fly much farther, stay in the air much longer, and carry a much heavier useful load. In late 1912, for instance, the first German naval Zeppelin made a flight of more than 30 hours duration, totalling 900 miles. Such performance could hardly be expected under service conditions, but even if the range and endurance of that flight were halved they were beyond the capabilities of any aeroplane in the world. The typical passenger load of the DELAG joy-rides was 20 persons, a weight impossible for any aeroplane of the period to lift – if that weight in humanity, why not that weight in bombs?

This question began to worry non-Teutonic Europe during the five years before World War I. Although a declaration of the Hague Conference of 1899 prohibited aerial bombardment, that proviso had expired in 1904, and the articles concerning bombardment of defended and undefended places embodied in the Land and Naval Warfare Conventions of the second Hague Conference of 1907 were contradictory and ambiguous. There was in fact nothing in international law to prevent aerial bombing of urban areas, and long before the war it was taken for granted that such attacks would occur in any future conflict.

Part of the Zeppelin's mystique was projected by German chauvinism. It was natural that patriotic pride would be manifested in a craft representing national leadership in science and technology; but there was more to it than that. David Lloyd George, travelling in Germany in 1908, caught a glimpse of that deeper emotion at its birth.

Hoping to see the flight of the Count's fourth ship, Great Britain's future prime minister arrived too late, to find a swarm of people viewing the wreckage in an 'agony of grief and dismay'. He wrote

> Hopes and ambitions far wider than those concerned with a scientific and mechanical success appeared to have shared the wreck of the dirigible. Then the crowd swung into the chanting of 'Deutschland über Alles' with a fanatic fervor of patriotism. What spearpoint of Imperial advance did this airship portend?[4]

A very far one indeed, the German masses soon came to believe. To them the Zeppelin became *the* symbol of Germany in the air, a gratifying example of national might. Unofficial and official propagandists, beating the drums for Germanic hegemony, were quick to exploit this emotion.

Lloyd George may have been the first Briton to apprehend the potential threat of the airship, but within a few years his qualms were shared by perhaps the majority of literate citizens in the

British Isles. The psychological impact of the Zeppelin upon British sensibilities is an important part of the background of the Cuxhaven Raid.

The beginning of the end of British insularity was heralded in 1909 with Louis Blériot's English Channel flight. If a puny aeroplane could bridge the moat that had sheltered Britain for centuries, it was obvious that the much farther-ranging airship could do so with ease. The Zeppelin bogey therefore began to take shape in 1910, and steadily over the next four years was fuelled with a growing imagination. Article after sensational article in the popular press fanned the fear ever higher. The titles of some of these, as listed by one writer, indicate their thrust: 'The Airship Menace', 'The Peril of the Air', 'The Black Shadow of the Airship', 'Britain's Peril in the Air', 'The New Terror', 'Germany: Lord of the Air'.[5] An especially vivid series of Zeppelin scare stories appeared in the *Review of Reviews* beginning in February 1913.

Other writers took up the cry. Karl Graves, self-styled former German secret agent, presented some frightening 'facts' in two prewar books. He described an aerial 'dreadnought' carrying 12 tons of bombs and remaining aloft for 96 hours, and other 'sky battleships' armed with 6 cannon and 7 tons of explosives, manned by a crew of 24 and with a range of 1180 kilometres. Graves dwelt at length on the havoc such craft could produce as they sailed the night skies over London.

The result of all this was an almost chronic 'Zeppelin craze' throughout Britain, similar to the 'flying saucer' crazes that have occurred periodically in North America since World War II, and with which it has been compared. Airships were 'seen' far and wide on nocturnal missions of frightening import. As early as 1910 a Zeppelin was believed to have appeared over London. During the next four years airships were reported over Sheerness, Portland, Dover and Liverpool, and twice over Cardiff. In one of the most celebrated instances, residents of Sheerness steadfastly maintained a Zeppelin had cruised over their city on the night of 14 October 1912.

This sort of thing was a type of mass hysteria produced by overwrought imaginations reacting to tricks of moonlight and cloud, the planet Venus, or even practical jokes. But through the miasma of half-truths, partially understood facts, and German propaganda, sober military and naval opinion began to perceive the airship as a serious threat.

This opinion was based not only on more reliable literature than the popular press, but on some firsthand experience. In 1911

Vivian Gaskell Blackburn in the pilot's seat of a Henri Farman on Mafia Island, German East Africa in July 1915, the month of the operation against SMS *Königsberg*. He flew a Type 74 in the Cuxhaven Raid with Chief Petty Officer James Bell as his observer. *Fleet Air Arm Museum*

Admiral Sir John Jellicoe, destined to be commander of the Grand Fleet during 1914-16, took a flight in one of the DELAG Zeppelins, accompanied by the British naval attaché in Berlin, and immediately became an advocate of the airship. In 1912, a subcommittee of the Committee of Imperial Defence despatched a two-man aeronautical fact-finding team to the Continent. The two, Mervyn O'Gorman, superintendent of the Royal Aircraft Factory, and a naval officer, Captain Murray F Sueter (of whom more later) also flew in a DELAG ship. Their report on German airship progress was extremely disquieting and, eventually, quite influential.

Agitation in the Royal Navy for an airship had begun in 1908 and was successfully shepherded through various layers of officialdom by the Admiralty's First Sea Lord, Admiral Sir John Fisher (Lord Fisher of Kilverstone, from November 1910). A contract for a rigid airship was given to Vickers, Sons and Maxim in 1909, and Sueter was named to head a small naval inspectorate to oversee its construction. Despite the care lavished on the design of this ship, popularly called *Mayfly*, it was probably inevitable that there would be defects in the first effort by a nation that lacked previous experience with rigids. And there were – upon completion in early 1911, the craft was too overweight to fly. Modifications were undertaken, but when the ship emerged from its shed on 24 September it was hit by a squall and totally wrecked under circumstances that are still not completely clear.[6]

A post-mortem on the disaster, held shortly after Winston Churchill became First Lord of the Admiralty, arrived at the recommendation that the navy abandon further work on rigid airships. But in the face of continued German progress, this decision was overturned within a few months. Further investigation of the rigid was authorized, one aspect of which was the O'Gorman–Sueter trip mentioned above. The findings of that tour furnished considerable ammunition for a later subcommittee report to the Committee of Imperial Defence that dwelt in detail on the advantages the rigid airship gave to Germany in a North Sea war. While stressing the value of aerial reconnaissance, the report also pointed out that the Zeppelins 'can certainly carry a sufficient weight of bombs to destroy torpedo-craft, dock gates, power stations, magazines, and the like'.[7]

The final result was a new and far more ambitious British airship programme calling for rigids and non-rigids to be built domestically and to be purchased abroad. But this effort came too late, the long 'lead time' required had been lost, and could not be regained before the coming of the war. Consequently, the Royal

Navy entered hostilities with only seven small non-rigids, useless for anything but short-range patrol scouting. The subsequent history of the muddled, confused British airship construction programme is beyond the scope of this story.[8] What is relevent is that for most of the war the British navy possessed nothing comparable to the Zeppelin, a deficiency that had a considerable influence upon the character of the North Sea struggle.

But, as noted at the beginning of this chapter, the major British concern as war clouds gathered in 1914 was not with the Zeppelin as an instrument of high seas reconnaissance but with its apparently more frightening role as a bomber.

This concern permeated nearly every level of military, naval and political officialdom. Winston Churchill, almost alone among British strategists, claims to have discounted the Zeppelin as a clumsy, ineffective, vulnerable weapon, carrying the seed of its destruction within it in the form of the highly flammable hydrogen that was its lifting agent. Such an 'enormous bladder of combustible and explosive gas', he was to declare 'would prove to be easily destructible'.[9] But this disclaimer was written years later, and, as the leading historian of the British rigid airship points out, must be read in the light of post-1916 events.[10] While Churchill vacillated greatly on the value of the rigid airship for British service, his words and actions as First Lord in 1914 make it obvious that he considered the rigid airship in German service a very serious threat indeed.

Churchill nevertheless took a more realistic view than many others in Britain. In some quarters outside the First Lord's office the quantity and quality of German airships were grossly exaggerated. The Zeppelins were reported bristling with quick-firing cannon, crammed with bombs, even capable of minelaying. They were thought to have practised bombing extensively. In a myth still not laid to rest, Germany was credited with a vast fleet of airships – 30 is the number often cited. It may be coincidental, but that is the number listed by a respected publication, Brassey's *Naval Annual*, in its 1913 edition, in which for the first time airships were given recognition. The figure was reached by lumping together every single German airship known to exist: army and navy, rigid and non-rigid, commercial and private, under the two headings 'battle airships' and 'minelaying and scouting airships'.[11]

There was little substance behind these British illusions. The German army airship branch had conducted exactly one experiment in the dropping of live bombs before the war. It entered hostilities with only seven operationally useable ships; far from carrying cannon, they were armed with only a machine gun or two; their early bombs were conventional shells with cloth streamers attached for stability. The faith placed in the Zeppelin by German populace and propagandists was not shared by the army staff, which mistrusted and misunderstood the craft. While there were some early attempts to use the army ships for bombing, they were so ineptly employed that three were lost to enemy ground fire in the first month of the war. The German army never really did find a use for the airship (although its craft took part in the later bombing campaign against Britain) and disbanded its airship branch in 1917 so that the increasingly scarce materials (such as rubber) it was devouring could be diverted to the more useful aeroplanes.[12]

Although the German navy expressed interest in the airship as early as 1906, that interest was blocked for the next six years, mainly by the Secretary of State for the Navy Office, Grossadmiral Alfred von Tirpitz. His objections were largely economic, for he resented diversion of funds from the battleships and torpedo craft that were the main elements of his 'risk navy'. But he had other qualms as well; for one thing, he did not believe the early airships, despite their range and endurance, were reliable enough to be of value to the fleet. 'As a naval officer who had got to know the force of the wind and the malice of squalls on sailing ships,' he was to write in his memoirs, 'I never promised myself much from the airships.'[13]

Tirpitz was finally pressured into acceptance of the airship in 1912; a lighter-than-air branch, called the Naval Airship Division, was established and a Zeppelin ordered. This ship, the L 1 (Luftschiff, or airship, No 1) made its first flight in October. A second and larger Zeppelin was ordered in 1913, and Tirpitz, finally yielding altogether, drew up plans for a five-year programme calling for ten Zeppelins (two squadrons of four each, with two ships in reserve), a large central airship base, and subsidisation of private airship sheds for wartime use.

But this ambitious effort was soon jeopardized by disaster. On 1 September 1913 the L 1 crashed at sea during a scouting exercise, killing 14 of its 20-man crew in the first loss of life in a Zeppelin accident. Only a few weeks later, on 17 October, the newly delivered L 2 was destroyed by explosion and fire in the air. All 28 aboard died.

This might well have been the end of the airship in the German navy. The five-year programme was abandoned (although work continued on the central base) and while the Naval Airship

Division remained in existence, its new commander, Korvetten-kapitän Peter Strasser (his predecessor had died in the *L1* disaster) was reduced to training crews on the DELAG ships. It was not until March 1914 that another Zeppelin was ordered for the navy; this ship, the *L3*, was delivered in May and was the only German naval airship in existence when war began in August, although a commercial Zeppelin was under navy charter for crew training.

The beginning of hostilities saw the rebirth of the Naval Airship Division. This occurred because of the High Sea Fleet's deficiency in scouting cruisers. The shortage was a legacy from Tirpitz, who, when laying the foundations of the modern German navy in the 1890s, had deprecated the cruiser as a craft having little value in a struggle with Britain. In his famous memorandum of June 1897 he wrote:

> Against England, indeed against any fleet penetrating our home waters, the value of scouting vessels is much reduced ... such vessels represent in a sense a reduction from the forces needed for the ultimate outcome.[14]

That belief may have been valid in 1897, when a British–German war might well have seen the Royal Navy attempting a close blockade of the German North Sea coast, but it was quite wrong in 1914, when the blockade was imposed in far waters, and the expanse of the North Sea rather than the coastal shallows became the naval battleground. The shortage of scouts became especially hindering when, after the stinging blow suffered in the Battle of the Heligoland Bight on 28 August 1914, the High Seas Fleet turned to a policy of guerrilla war, attempting to whittle down the enemy battleline by traps and ambushes. Only when these tactics had succeeded in bringing the High Seas Fleet to parity with or superiority over British dreadnought strength, was a major action to be risked. Adequate means of reconnaissance were essential to this policy. Yet the table of organization of the High Seas Fleet at the start of the war shows only six light cruisers available for scouting duty.

Fortuitously, just when the cruiser deficiency was becoming felt, the Zeppelin was there to fill the gap as a craft that could be produced in a fraction of the time required to build a cruiser and at a fraction of the cost. Consequently, within a few weeks from the start of hostilities the Imperial Navy embarked on a high-priority programme of construction of airships and airship bases. Bases were as important as ships, for the Zeppelins were fragile giants, highly vulnerable to wind and weather, requiring huge hangars in which to shelter from the elements.

The time required to get this project underway, plus an inevitable amount of bureaucratic muddle, caused initial delay, and by the end of 1914 the navy had commissioned only five new Zeppelins (plus acquiring three non-rigids of considerably less operational value) and none of the new bases had been completed.[15]

Nor were the naval Zeppelins yet prepared for combat. Although their use in the bombing role had been discussed before the war, they were even less equipped for it than the army airships. They did not receive their first bombs until October, and so little provision had been made for them that at first they were simply slung from cords that were cut with a knife to release them.

But none of these weaknesses and deficiencies of the German lighter-than-air forces was known to the British when the guns of August roared out. The Zeppelins remained in British minds menacing 'monsters of the purple twilight', (as one writer has called them, paraphrasing Tennyson[16]), certain soon to spring from their lairs and unleash a torrent of death and destruction.

CHAPTER 2

Distressing Their Ships Within Their Havens

B ut the monsters did not stray far from their lairs. That was hardly surprising, in view of their actual feebleness. What is surprising is that agitation for airship bombardment of Britain began in some quarters of the German navy as early as August, long before the Naval Airship Division possessed the strength, equipment or experience for such an effort.

An early exponent was Konteradmiral Paul Behncke, deputy chief of the naval staff, and he was soon seconded by Konterad-miral Philipp, who in late August became chief of naval air forces. Even Tirpitz, isolated from operational conduct of the fleet by the peculiar fragmented organization of the Imperial Navy hierarchy, took up the cry.

The target of their arguments, Admiral Hugo von Pohl, chief of the naval staff, was initially unwilling to divert the airships from their mission of maritime scouting, especially while so few ships existed. Not only would the High Seas Fleet be losing the services of valuable instruments of reconnaissance, but there were not enough airships to achieve much effect. Advocates of bombing countered by arguing that numerical strength could be aug-mented by obtaining the co-operation of the army airship branch.

Von Pohl was finally persuaded of the merits of a bombing campaign, but efforts to launch it encountered immediate resistance in the person of Kaiser Wilhelm II, whose authorization as 'Supreme War Lord' was required. What is reported to have been one of his objections has a quaintly old-fashioned ring: as a grandson of Queen Victoria, he was worried about offending or harming his relatives in the British royal family if London, the most logical and most inviting target, were bombed. The truth is that he was concerned about the effect on world opinion, which had already unleashed a torrent of opprobrium against Germany for the invasion of Belgium.

During the autumn months, as a few more naval airships became available, suggestions for a joint army–navy bombing effort were broached. Still nothing was done; the issue remained mired in 'Luftpolitik', as the leading historian of the Naval Airship Division has called it.[1]

The British, unwitting beneficiaries of this vacillation, puzzled by the absence of Zeppelin attack on their homeland but convinced of its inevitability, remained apprehensive. Anxiety increased when on 24 August and 2 September 1914, German army airships bombed Antwerp by night, killing about a dozen people and injuring a larger number. The Zeppelins grew ever more menacing in the imagination. In late October, for example, one of the war-spawned weekly publications described supposed experiments in which a Zeppelin cruised over Lake Constance every night for six weeks, dropping missiles 'with great precision and rapidity'.[2] The illustrators of this and other publications filled page after page with drawings of Zeppelin armadas. But lest the dire predictions prove too frightening, the popular press also began to note the ways in which airships were vulnerable and to describe, or dream up, weapons and tactics to combat them.

As the bright late summer and early autumn months wore on, bringing clear moon-lit nights with ideal flying conditions for the airships, defensive measures were indeed being taken in advance of the expected blow. The burden of these measures fell on the Admiralty's aerial branch, the Royal Naval Air Service.

This branch had begun existence in 1912 as the Naval Wing of the newly established Royal Flying Corps, but quickly took on a quasi-independence from the parent organization, and was made nominally official one month before Britain went to war. The air service became a special pet of Winston Churchill, who took over as First Lord in late 1911. Churchill had a strong personal interest in aviation, took flying instruction, and, it is said, gave it up before becoming a fully qualified aviator only because of objections from government and family that it was too dangerous and undignified for a First Lord to go chasing about in flying machines. In his official position he fostered the prewar growth of the RNAS and, with his lifelong love of gadgetry, encouraged such technical innovations as the torpedo plane, the folding wing and the flotation bag. Although in a last-minute change of heart Churchill had opposed the separation of the naval and military air wings, preferring a unified air service,[3] he was quick to expand and utilize the RNAS after war began.

In fact, under his aegis the aerial branch became almost an independent national armed service, a combination air force, navy and army. By the time he left office in May 1915 the RNAS was not only flying landplanes, seaplanes, airships and kite balloons, it was commanding and manning seaplane carriers, balloon ships and motor launches, and on dry land was operating armoured car squadrons, kite balloon sections, batteries of anti-aircraft guns and searchlights, motorcycle machine-gun units, and armoured trains. It was functioning in Britain, France, Belgium, Egypt, East Africa, Mesopotamia, the Aegean islands and Gallipoli. There was a certain wry truth to the quip that the initials RNAS stood for 'Really Not A Sailor'.

In its wildfire growth during the first ten months of the war the air service took on, much to the chagrin of some high-ranking naval officers, many of the qualities characterizing the semi-irregular corps that seem to have sprung up in all of Britain's wars – tendencies to chafe at discipline, experiment with unconventional weapons and tactics, and hare off to fight private battles. In several ways it resembled nothing so much as the semi-piratical Elizabethan navy, with all the courage, sturdiness, skill and damn-your-eyes independence of Francis Drake's and John Hawkins' cut-throats.

The administrative chief of this outfit, and during the early war months often its *de facto* operational commander, was Captain (later Rear Admiral Sir) Murray Frazer Sueter, mentioned earlier as head of the *Mayfly* inspectorate. He had joined the inspectorate after pioneering work in submarines and radio, and following the airship fiasco went on to occupy the top post in the infant Royal Naval Air Service. In 1914 he bore the title of Director, Air Department – DAD under the British penchant for addressing officers by the initials of their staff titles, and a singularly apt pun involving a man who has so often been called the father of British naval aviation.

Several interlocking factors resulted in Sueter's service shouldering the main burden of Britain's aerial defence, but the most important was the fact that by the end of August 1914 nearly every operational aircraft and trained aviator of the Royal Flying Corps (the name retained by the army's air branch after separation of the two wings) had been sent to France with the British Expeditionary Force. This threw into abeyance a system of joint RFC–RNAS defensive patrols that had been drawn up a few months before the war and put into effect in early August. With the RFC quickly strained to its meagre limits in support of the hard-pressed BEF and with only a training cadre of army airmen left in Britain, these patrols became almost entirely a naval responsibility.[4]

This early system of passive patrolling around areas considered the most likely landfalls of raiding airships was unproductive and tedious, 'there was not much to report, and it was weary work waiting for the enemy to begin'[5], but it was soon superseded by a more offensive policy.

The change of policy began on 3 September, the eve of the Battle of the Marne*, with a request to Churchill by Lord Kitchener, Secretary of State for War, that the Admiraly take over the entire aerial defence of Britain; the First Lord assented. A result of that assent was to burden the RNAS with what eventually became a vast apparatus of ground defence (guns, searchlights, warning stations) from which it would not become disentangled until early 1916. This system had to be created virtually from scratch; there was, for instance, no more than a handful of true anti-aircraft guns in the entire United Kingdom in September 1914.

But Churchill realized

> it was no use sitting down and waiting for a year while these [defensive] preparations were completing. Only offensive action could help us. I decided immediately to strike, by bombing from aeroplanes, at the Zeppelin sheds wherever these gigantic structures could be found in Germany.[6]

This concept was far from original; an Admiralty committee had made a virtually identical recommendation before the war. Nonetheless, these sentences reveal two interesting and important points. The first is that Churchill was reapplying in a new dimension, the air, a fundamental tenet of British maritime strategy – that the defence of Britain best begins at the highwater mark of the nearest enemy port. This concept dated from Elizabethan days, when in 1587 Francis Drake, setting out for the first of his beard-singeing expeditions against Philip II, was authorized to 'impeach the purpose of the Spanish fleet' even if it required 'distressing their ships within their havens'.

This simple but important idea – defence by means of offence, striking the enemy on his home territory before he can reach your own – became a key principle of British naval policy during the long series of French wars. Not always clearly articulated, at times appreciated more viscerally than intellectually, sometimes brilliantly executed (as at Quiberon Bay in 1759), sometimes bungled (as at Aix Roads in 1809), it remained traditionally the most

---

* And coincidentally, 16 years and one day after the Battle of Omdurman, on the eve of which, according to his own account, Churchill had been the first to bring cavalry reconnaissance reports of the Dervish army to Kitchener.

effective way of keeping an enemy from British soil. Its importance was as clearly understood by Churchill in 1914 as it had been
by Elizabeth I's naval advisers in 1587.

The second point revealed by Churchill related to tactics and
technology rather than strategy, and shows that his policy of
countering the Zeppelins was dicated as much by the state of
aerial weaponry in 1914 as it was by the tradition of the offensive.
While Churchill was ultimately correct in his judgement that the
hydrogen airship would prove highly vulnerable to the aeroplane, there was really no way in 1914 to exploit that vulnerability
in aerial combat. This was true even for the Royal Naval Air
Service, which before the war had experimented with aircraft
armament more than any other air arm in the world and was
relatively better equipped to deal with the Zeppelins than the
Royal Flying Corps, whose prewar thinking had centred more on
the use of aircraft for reconnaissance than combat.

Much of that experimentation had been with the Zeppelin in
mind, and the naval fliers had tried out machine guns, rifles with
incendiary ammunition, small-calibre cannon, shotguns firing
chain shot, flare pistols and rifle grenades. The war years would
bring explosive darts, rockets, and probably the most bizarre
weapon of all – the Fiery Grapnel, an air-to-air missile equipped
with anchor-like hooks to fasten it to an airship's outer fabric
while its explosive contents did their deadly work.

But none of these proved effective; the Zeppelin's fate was not
sealed until the introduction of special incendiary and explosive
machine-gun bullets in 1916.* Until then the airship, so easily
turned by the slightest spark into a cauldron of white-hot hell,
was paradoxically almost inviolable in the air. But that immunity
ended on the ground, where sheltering immobile in their huge
sheds, the airships were at the mercy of aeroplanes dropping
bombs** and so it was there, rather than in the skies, that
Churchill logically chose to strike at them.

* Actually, the airships were always vulnerable to incendiaries. But the British,
in a piece of self-deception that crippled anti-airship efforts for nearly two years,
believed the highly flammable hydrogen cells were protected by an outer
sheathing that was filled by an inert gas or by gasses fed from the airships'
engine exhausts, in either case providing an incendiary-quenching barrier.
There was no truth in this belief, whose origin seems impossible to trace. To
penetrate this supposed protection, the machine guns of the first anti-airship
aeroplanes employed interspersed rounds of explosive bullets (to blow apart the
outer covering), incendiaries (to ignite the hydrogen after passing through the
gaps torn by the explosives), and tracer (to assist aiming).

** Theoretically, they were equally vulnerable to bombing while in flight. But
despite the size of a Zeppelin, it was a difficult target for an aeroplane to hit with

The Admiralty had a weapon already in position on the Continent to start the anti-Zeppelin campaign – the RNAS Eastchurch Squadron (later redesignated No 3 Squadron). This comprised a heterogeneous collection of ten landplanes under the command of the dashing, and soon to be highly publicized, Wing Commander Charles Rumney Samson. He was one of the Royal Navy's first four aviators, a prewar pioneer of deck take-off, seaplane and night flying, bombing and aerial radio, and a man who bore, appropriately, a considerable physical resemblance to Francis Drake, beard and all. On 27 August this unit had been sent to Ostend to support a Royal Marine brigade landed there, in a feint intended to draw German pressure off the British Expeditionary Force and Belgian army. At the end of this three-day diversion the squadron withdrew to Dunkirk in preparation for returning to England but was delayed in the French port by the crash of one of its planes. On 1 September Samson received an order from the Admiralty directing the squadron to stay at Dunkirk to operate against enemy aircraft and co-operate with French ground forces.*

It is possible this order stemmed from French requests that the squadron remain, (appeals unmentioned by Churchill in his account of events) rather than being an anticipation of Kitchener's request of two days later. The effect was in either case the same, for both an Admiralty message of 1 September to the French Ministry of Marine and a Churchill memo of 5 September citing the Admiralty's new and enlarged aerial defence responsibilities state that aircraft at Dunkirk would endeavour to gain control of the air for a radius of a hundred miles around the city, attacking Zeppelins wherever they might appear within that circle.[7]

That the First Lord's campaign of distressing the airships in their havens did pre-date Kitchener's request, however, is

---

a bomb while it was mobile. In addition, the aeroplanes of the early war years often had trouble attaining the altitude advantage this tactic required, for the airship had a very high rate of climb. Of the many German airships lost in the war, only one, the army's *LZ 37*, was destroyed by bombing in the air.

* A consequence of this was the introduction of the armoured car into Britain's armed forces. Samson improvised a couple of such cars to fight off roving parties of cavalry; Churchill, impressed by these vehicles, had improved versions produced, and soon the RNAS was operating squadrons of them. Most of the Eastchurch Squadron's fighting in 1914 was done on the ground from armoured cars until their utility vanished with the beginnings of the static trench system at Ypres. The vehicles' inability to function in' those circumstances, plus their earlier difficulty in coping with rough terrain, led to the research that eventually produced the tank; research in which Sueter played an important part.

indicated by the fact that on 3 September, the day of that request, three RNAS planes arrived at Ostend prior to moving to Antwerp for operation there against Zeppelin sheds in Germany. But nine days later, while arrangements for them were being made at Antwerp, they were destroyed by a storm and the Eastchurch Squadron was required to replace them from its dwindling number of aircraft.

The first attack was made from Antwerp on 22 September with raids of two planes each on Düsseldorf and Cologne. Because of bad weather, only one pilot could find his target and the bombs he aimed at the Düsseldorf hangar were ineffective.

On 3 October the rest of the Eastchurch Squadron moved north to assist the Royal Naval Division, which was resisting what was now a full-scale German drive on Antwerp. Five days later, in the midst of a panicky civilian evacuation of the bombarded city, flying from a field in imminent danger from German artillery, two planes tried again. One pilot was unable to find his target at Cologne, but the other destroyed the army Zeppelin *Z IX* at Düsseldorf. Both pilots returned just in time to join the withdrawal of the Eastchurch Squadron, now down to four servicable planes, from Antwerp.[8]

That withdrawal ended the anti-airship effort in the north, but the next month a special four-plane RNAS unit was sent to Belfort in extreme eastern France to strike at the very heart of the German lighter-than-air industry, the Luftschiffbau Zeppelin works at Friedrichshafen on Lake Constance. The raid they carried out on 21 November was thought to have destroyed or badly damaged one airship and inflicted heavy damage on the plant, but in fact did neither.

This attack brought to an end the first land phase of Churchill's anti-airship campaign – never really a campaign in the sense of the sustained, co-ordinated British strategic bombing effort of World War II (although the Friedrichshafen raid required considerable planning and preparation) but basically *ad hoc*.[9] Although its results were meagre, the British were heartened, believing they had achieved more than later knowledge would show. The Zeppelin had lost some of its aura of mystery and frightfulness and morale was lifted. Churchill's announcement of the Friedrichshafen raid in the House of Commons caused a stir nearly comparable to his more memorable addresses one war later.

The fact remained that for the RNAS units on the Continent, the campaign was over for 1914. The German army's advance into western and southern Belgium after the fall of Antwerp placed the airship bases in central interior Germany beyond the effective range of any aeroplane possessed by the Admiralty, and the Friedrichshafen raid, carried out at what was then extreme long range and undertaken only at the risk of violating Swiss air space, was never repeated because of protests about that violation.[10]

But while the fliers ashore had been straining to get at the airships from Belgium and France, their comrades in Britain had been planning and attempting a comparable blow. Their target was the heart of the Naval Airship Division, the big base the British believed was at Cuxhaven. Their efforts, baffled and frustrated during the autumn months of 1914 by a series of delays and failures, would climax in the Cuxhaven Raid.

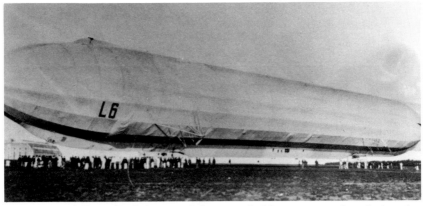

German naval Zeppelin *L 6*, one of the two airships to see action during the Cuxhaven Raid. She is shown at the Nordholz base, the revolving hangar is partially visible in the left background. *By courtesy of Dr Douglas H Robinson*

CHAPTER 3

The Aerial Game

Proposals for an aerial attack on the German coast were put forward at the Admiralty during the earliest days of the war, although the suggested targets were not airship bases but the Kaiser Wilhelm (Kiel) Canal and the German fleet base at Wilhelmshaven.

On the very first day of hostilities (presumably 5 August*) Claude Grahame-White, probably the most famous prewar British aviator, reportedly approached Churchill with a plan for a raid on the Kiel Canal. According to Grahame-White's biographer, who is the only source for the story, the flier volunteered the services of himself and some fellow civilian pilots who would equip their own planes with floats for embarkation on two destroyers that would carry them into German waters under cover of darkness. Taking off at dawn, the aircraft would bomb a lock-gate and any shipping they could find in the canal and then return to the destroyers.[1] The story states that Churchill was impressed with the idea and recommended it to Sueter, but that officer immediately scotched it as impractical.

The official British air history states that a proposal for an aerial sortie against the canal and Wilhelmshaven was advanced on 13 August. This may have been an official presentation of the Grahame-White plan or a totally different suggestion, but in either case it proved abortive because, according to the official history, 'the machinery was too imperfect'.[2]

---

* The date is in doubt because of the backdating to 4 August of the British declaration of war on Germany officially announced at 12.15am 5 August, the British ultimatum having expired 15 minutes earlier. Thus the first day of hostilities has often been given as 4 August when in fact it was 5 August. It is difficult to believe that Grahame-White, despite his fame and personal acquaintance with Churchill, could have obtained an appointment with the First Lord on that tumultous first day of war, but more reasonable to suppose that he could have the previous day.

That phrase may be interpreted in a number of ways, but the great barrier to such an attack was the lack of the requisite aircraft–surface ship combination. The attack would, of course, have to be from the sea, since geographically the target area was beyond the reach of any aeroplane flying from Britain, Belgium or France. An attack from the sea would have to be by seaplane, for although there had been several prewar Royal Navy experiments in flying landplanes from special platforms or ramps aboard ships, this was a tricky technique very much in its infancy and could not be relied upon under service conditions.

It might have been thought, as it apparently was by Grahame-White, that it would be a simple matter to place a seaplane aboard a warship which could then carry it to any desired take-off point. This could be done, and would be innumerable times during World War I, but the Royal Navy had learned during prewar experiments that it was not as simple as it appeared, that efficient, reliable operation of seaplanes from ships required special features few warships possessed. These included a relatively large, unencumbered deck area for aircraft accommodation, extra-long handling booms to prevent fragile wings from being crushed through brushing against hull or superstructure during hoisting-out and recovery from the water, and some form of shelter to protect aircraft from damage by wind and wave.

These lessons had been learned largely from operation of the old cruiser *Hermes* as a seaplane carrier during and for several weeks after the fleet manoeuvres of 1913, the longest and most sustained test of shipboard aviation conducted by any navy before World War I. As a result of the *Hermes* experiment, the Royal Navy had in 1914 acquired an incomplete merchant hull for conversion into the world's first specialized aviation vessel, a ship that would gain fame under the name *Ark Royal* and pass that name along to an even more famous aircraft carrier of World War II.

But *Ark Royal* was far from complete when the war began (she was not commissioned until December 1914) and the only thing resembling an aviation vessel then possessed by the Royal Navy was the old *Hermes*, still partially equipped with the aircraft facilities installed in 1913 but capable of operating only two seaplanes at the most (she would be used as an air service transport until sunk by a submarine in October).

This deficiency began to be remedied, however, on the very day (13 August) that the machinery for an aero-naval attack on Germany was ruled too imperfect, with the commissioning into the navy of two ships destined to be the nucleus of what by 1918 would be the world's largest force of aviation vessels.

These were the passenger packets *Engadine* and *Riviera*, acquired two days earlier from the South-Eastern and Chatham Railway Company whose cross-channel routes they had served in peace-time. They were turbine-driven, 313-foot sisters completed in 1911, of 1678 and 1675 tons, respectively, and capable of at least 21 knots. Also acquired the same day from the same company was the similar, but older (1907) and slower (18-knot) packet *Empress* of 1694 tons.[3]

HMS *Riviera*, one of the three seaplane carriers of the Cuxhaven Raid, as she appeared in early war rig with canvas aircraft shelters fore and aft. *Engadine* was nearly identical in appearance, and *Empress* very similar. Remodelling in 1915 replaced the canvas screens with a large aft hangar. *Imperial War Musuem*

Engadine and *Riviera* were crudely but quickly converted to seaplane carriers at Chatham dockyard in work that began on 18 August. When that work was completed near the end of the month, they did not feature the large box-like steel hangars that characterized them and other British seaplane carriers later in the war; instead, they were fitted with simple canvas screens on forecastle and quarterdeck that could be unfurled to shelter three seaplanes (one forward, two aft). Installation of long handling booms, a couple of 12-pounder guns and interior facilities for storage of aircraft fuel and spare parts completed the transformation. *Engadine* completed first and on 1 September proceeded to Sheerness to embark seaplanes from the Isle of Grain RNAS station, followed a few days later by *Riviera*.

Empress, meanwhile, commissioned at Chatham on 25 August as an air service transport and supply vessel. Two days later she and the collier *Rawcliffe* took the ground equipment and ground personnel of the Eastchurch Squadron to Ostend. Soon after this

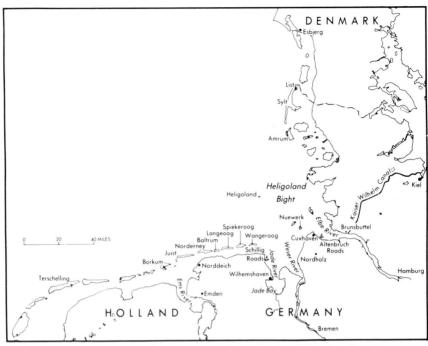

The north German coast and German (East) Frisian Islands, showing geographical points of importance to the Cuxhaven Raid including main High Seas Fleet anchorages at Schillig Roads and Altenbruch Roads. *Map by Bruce Krefting*

Empress was replaced for RNAS transport work by the merchantman *Princess Victoria* and on 8 September entered Chatham dockyard for conversion to a seaplane carrier along the lines of *Engadine* and *Riviera*. She followed them to Sheerness on 10 October.

The original purpose in converting these vessels was to provide aerial eyes for the Grand Fleet, and it had been intended to send them to Scapa Flow to join the main elements of that fleet under Admiral Sir John Jellicoe (later Viscount Jellicoe of Scapa). Channel packets were chosen for this role because their speed (much greater than other types of merchant vessels except ocean liners) would permit them to keep pace with the Battle Fleet.[4] But instead they went south, to join the Harwich Force with a view to their use against airships. The change of plan can reasonably be assumed a result of Churchill's decision to mount the anti-Zeppelin campaign, although documentation of that assertion is lacking.

The Harwich Force, named after the port in which it was based, had been established on the first day of the war to control the expanse of sea from Britain to the Continent between the 52nd and 54th parallels. It was commanded by one of the finest Royal

Navy officers in history, Commodore (later Admiral of the Fleet Sir) Reginald Yorke Tyrwhitt. The force's ships were continually at sea, in all weather, from the first day of hostilities to the last, protecting British maritime interests and constantly hectoring and harassing the Germans. Its waters, more than any other sea, constituted the true 'front line' of the naval war.

Although organically a part of the Grand Fleet, the Harwich Force was under the direct control of the Admiralty except when it sortied north of the 54th parallel and then came under Jellicoe's command. Tyrwhitt, however, could and did exercise a good deal of independence.

The strength of the force fluctuated, but in mid-October, shortly after the seaplane carriers joined, it consisted of four light cruisers, the new *Arethusa* class sisters *Arethusa* (Tyrwhitt's flagship), *Aurora* and *Undaunted*, plus the older 'scout' *Fearless*, and the First and Third Flotillas averaging twenty destroyers each. *Undaunted* served as flagship of the Third Flotilla and *Fearless* of the First. This strength remained fairly stable through early 1915.

Also based at Harwich was the Eighth (Oversea) Submarine Flotilla under an officer who would equal Tyrwhitt in fame, Commodore (later Admiral of the Fleet Sir) Roger Keyes. Keyes was also the Royal Navy's overall commander of the submarine force. The Harwich flotilla was originally composed of 10 boats of the 'E' and 'D' classes, largest and longest-ranged of prewar British submarines. Because prewar submarine doctrine envisioned multiple numbers of undersea craft acting under control of a surface flagship, two destroyers were attached to the flotilla as command vessels, *Lurcher* (flying Keyes' flag) and *Firedrake*. The destroyers also served as radio linking vessels, since the only radio transmitters that could be carried on the early submarines lacked the range to reach Britain from positions far out in the North Sea.

Tyrwhitt and Keyes had worked in harness since the start of the war. They were an excellent combination, both aggressive, capable and efficient. Both had played conspicuous parts in the 28 August Battle of the Heligoland Bight, when despite bad staff work and faulty communications the Royal Navy had inflicted a blistering defeat on the High Seas Fleet by sinking three cruisers and a destroyer. Both would play equally conspicuous roles in the Cuxhaven Raid.

If there was an exact date on which Churchill decided to extend the spoiling campaign against the Zeppelins by attacking the Naval Airship Division's main base from the sea, it is not recorded. The decision to send the newly converted carriers to Harwich instead of Scapa Flow indicates he may have had the plan in mind for late September or early October, and the attempt might have been made earlier had various factors not intervened. There was bound to be some initial delay while the crews of the carriers and their planes practiced to gain experience in the novel and tricky techniques of launching and recovering aircraft at sea.

But probably more contributory to delay were events on the land front. During early October the concern of the Admiralty was focused on Antwerp, where a Marine brigade and the raw troops of the Royal Naval Division were trying to fend off the German onslaught. Churchill himself was in the threatened city in early October, a visit that resulted in his quixotic offer to resign as First Lord and take command of the defence. Later in the month the so-called Race to the Sea climaxed with the start of the struggle that would complete the destruction of Britain's prewar professional army, the 'Old Contemptibles', the survivors of Mons, Le Cateau, the Marne and the Aisne – the protracted clash that history has labelled the First Battle of Ypres.

The Royal Navy was no mere onlooker during these events. A strong inshore squadron co-operated with and covered the left flank of the Allied forces trying to stem the German advance down the Belgian coast after the fall of Antwerp. The Harwich Force was intensely involved with protecting and supporting this squadron, too intensely to spare ships or time for an aerial operation even if the Admiralty had been inclined to one. It was not until the enemy advance was beginning to be slowed just north of Dunkirk, where the trench lines would remain unmoved for the next four years, that a breathing space occurred.

Plans for an aero-naval blow at the Zeppelins were formulated toward the end of October. On the 22nd, Tyrwhitt, only hours ashore after a gruelling stint at sea, was summoned to the Admiralty for the planning session. Also present at this conference were Churchill; the First Sea Lord, Admiral Prince Louis of Battenberg (later Admiral of the Fleet the Marquess of Milford Haven); and the Chief of the Naval Staff, Vice Admiral Sir Doveton Sturdee. Sueter, strangely enough, was absent.[5]

The operational plan that emerged from this meeting was based on one tried unsuccessfully by the Harwich Force earlier in the month as a purely surface raid. It called for Tyrwhitt to penetrate the Heligoland Bight to a point near the island of Heligoland, where the carriers, protected by cruisers and destroyers, would launch seaplanes. Meanwhile, *Fearless* and the First Flotilla would operate farther west, off the mouth of the Ems River, to pick off any isolated German patrol vessels they might find. Distant support would be given by the newly formed Second Battle Cruiser Squadron (the 12-inch gunned *Inflexible* and *Invincible*), which with a division of destroyers would steam from Cromarty, base of Vice Admiral Sir David Beatty's battlecruiser force. It is difficult to determine whether such a deep penetration into German waters with such a slender supporting force should be characterized as daring or foolhardy.

It is likely that this conference was the first time the target of the aerial attack was labelled 'Cuxhaven', the name used ever since in reference to the raid as finally carried out. Actually, the British did not know the exact site of the airship base, only that it was somewhere in proximity to the coastal city. It was in fact eight miles south, near the inland village of Nordholz, separated from Cuxhaven by a stretch of fertile, heavily cultivated orchard land although the base itself was close to a wooded area. It had been chosen by a joint navy-civilian site selection committee as the location for an airship base even before the naval lighter-than-air programme of 1913 had been authorized and its initial development had been done so unobtrusively, if not downright secretly, that until December 1912 the British believed it was to be a rifle range.

Weather conditions were luckily favourable enough to permit the operation to be mounted only two days after it was planned. The Harwich Force sailed at 5am on 24 October for a sortie that would take it through the most dangerous waters under cover of night, to reach the seaplane take-off position approximately 24 hours later, at dawn on the 25th. But the luck with the weather did not last. Conditions worsened during the night, and dawn brought fog and what the British air history calls 'a deluge of rain'[6] that made take-off impossible. The same fog and rain, however, screened the British force from Zeppelin *L 4*, patrolling west of the Friesian Islands that morning. To the south, *Fearless* and her destroyers could sight nothing. The entire operation had been a futile exercise so course was shaped for home.

Tyrwhitt, who had entertained high hopes for this novel form of attack, was deeply disappointed, bitterly and unfairly blaming 'those idiots' of the air service for the failure and declaring himself 'sick to death of everything connected with aviation'.[7] These were strange words from an officer who would later make such progressive and innovative use of shipboard aviation. But this was Tyrwhitt's first experience with an aero-naval combination, and his knowledge of both the capabilities and frailties of aircraft was at this stage probably close to zero.

In gleaming prewar light colour scheme, the German battleship SMS *Wettin* in transit through the Kaiser Wilhelm (Kiel) Canal. Her shots mistakenly fired at a German trawler were the first of the Cuxhaven Raid and the only ones to be aimed by one surface ship against another. *US Naval Photographic Center*

Perhaps some such knowledge was imparted to him by Churchill during an interview on 27 October in which the failure was discussed. At any rate, Tyrwhitt emerged from this meeting quite mollified, cheerfully professing eagerness to repeat what he now called the aerial 'game'.

Churchill, too, was disappointed at the failure, but as one considerably more knowledgable about aircraft, fully understood the reason for it. Basically it was due to the inherent handicaps the seaplane* faced in flying from the element it was designed to take off from. The seaplane was quite a new development in 1914; the first British seaplane had flown only three years before. Although its improvement had been rapid, as technical development often was in the early days of aviation, there were unsolved problems. The chief of these was simply the difficulty the craft had in getting into the air from the water. Take-off was difficult to impossible in rough seas, high wind, rain, or any combination of these. Perversely, the reverse of these conditions, a dead calm and/or a flat sea, could also thwart take-off, for then it was difficult or impossible for the plane to break the surface suction straining to keep its floats in the water.

Planes taking off on wheels from flat surfaces did not, of course, face these handicaps, and this is essentially the reason the flight-deck aircraft carrier came into existence. It was this realization that inspired Churchill, immediately after the 25 October failure, to a technical brainstorm of the kind with which he bedevilled subordinates in two wars. In a memo to Sueter the next day, he advocated launching planes from long barges, either by take-off on detachable wheel undercarriages which would be dropped after flight was achieved, or by an 'accelerating windlass' activating a rail-mounted trolley. Upon returning from their mission, the aircraft would ditch alongside friendly ships, relying on flotation gear to keep them on the surface long enough for their crews to be picked up. Sacrifice of the aircraft and even scuttling of the barges would be acceptable if results could be achieved. In a typical Churchillian imperative, the First Lord directed Sueter to get started on such a project that very day.[8]

It is going too far to claim, as one writer has, that this memo contains the genesis of the aircraft carrier,[9] for that concept had been broached and discussed in the Royal Navy and elsewhere much earlier. But it did presage two other lines of shipboard aviation development. The 'accelerating windlass' foreshadowed

* Churchill coined the name seaplane to replace the cumbersome word hydroaeroplane.

the catapult, which the Royal Navy had considered before the war but did not begin to develop until 1917, while the aircraft barge plan was prescient of the high-speed towed aircraft lighters that the Harwich Force would operate in 1918.

Churchill's proposal was feasible enough technically, but its implementation would have required a period of development and experimentation that might have lasted for months. Such a delay was unacceptable unless the Cuxhaven Raid were to be shelved indefinitely, and with the airship menace still apparently imminent there was no intention of doing that. It was probably the indefinite postponment of the raid the Churchill proposal would have entailed that caused Sueter to sidestep the matter. How he managed that tactful manoeuvre is not recorded, but the plan sinks from sight after its one appearance.

There were too many delaying factors already. The principal one was the weather, which as the blustery North Sea autumn wore on became increasingly crucial to planning the next attempt at a sea-borne air raid. A repeat of the thwarted operation was scheduled twice during the next few weeks, in late October and in early November, but both times had to be cancelled because of adverse weather before a single anchor was weighed.

Important as the weather was, there were other causes for delay. The Harwich Force was continually engaged in a myriad of vital activities which could not be dropped immediately the wind turned fair for Germany, and larger events interfered. Only the day after Tyrwhitt's meeting with Churchill, Prince Louis resigned as First Sea Lord, pressured out of office ostensibly by a public and press campaign of unjust villification of his German ancestry and connections, but in fact probably more because influential naval and political circles considered him too languid in conduct of the naval war and too much of a rubber-stamp for the civilian First Lord.[10]

He was succeeded by Lord Fisher, returning from retirement to the post he had resigned from in 1910. Experienced as Fisher was in that office, such a change of command inevitably brings an adminstrative upheaval during which operations often get momentarily neglected. And only three days after Fisher took office the main attention of the Admiralty had to be turned half a world away when the Royal Navy suffered its worst setback yet of the war with the destruction of a cruiser squadron off Coronel on the Chilean coast. The planning of measures to counter this success of the German Pacific Squadron took on urgent priority.

And so, notwithstanding Tyrwhitt's eagerness to replay the aerial game, the whims of weather, the exigencies of North Sea naval war, the complexities of administrative change and the demands of global maritime strategy combined to postpone the next attempt at a Cuxhaven Raid for a full month.

With the next effort, a new element was added by Admiralty planners: an attempt to entice the High Seas Fleet into battle by using the Harwich Force as bait. Unlike the October operation, which had been supported by only two battlecruisers, this time the expedition would be backed by the main units of the Grand Fleet standing by (although at a considerable distance) to fall upon any German force that might be lured out by the presence of the carriers and their escorts. The attack on the airship base was still definitely part of the scheme, but would be secondary to the main objective of setting the stage for a fleet action on terms favourable to Jellicoe.

An Admiralty message of 20 November to Jellicoe told him of a 'concentration of German cruisers, battlecruisers and battleships in Weser and Elbe estuaries and ... disposal of their submarines to hunt in the Shetlands and English Channel.'[11] It will be noted from this message that Admiralty intelligence was already becoming proficient at ascertaining enemy dispositions through deciphering intercepted radio signals. This technique was made possible by the good fortune that preserved three copies of the principal German naval codebook on the cruiser *Magdeburg* when she was wrecked in the Baltic in September. One of these invaluable volumes had been made available to the Admiralty on 13 October after the cruiser HMS *Theseus* had made a special voyage to north Russia to pick it up.

The 20 November message continued,

> In these favourable circumstances, the aerial attack on Cuxhaven Zeppelin bases, which we had previously planned and considered desirable in itself, might easily bring on a considerable action in which your battlecruisers and the Grand Fleet might take part without undue risk of German submarines.[12]

Such reassurance about submarine risk was essential to persuade Jellicoe to order a major fleet movement, for he had frankly told the Admiralty earlier that he would refuse to commit the fleet to action under any condition that threatened to expose it to underwater attack.

The new aim of the Cuxhaven operation was further emphasized the next day in another message to Jellicoe after he had requested a 24-hour delay to permit completion of some repairs: 'The seaplane attack is incidental and subsidiary, though very desirable in itself. It may bring on an action ...' It concluded by timing the seaplane attack for 5.30am on 24 November.[13]

Jellicoe was prepared to act the next day, and the operation began at dusk on 22 November with the sailing from its various bases of the bulk of the Grand Fleet: The First, Second, Third and Fourth Battle Squadrons, First Battle Cruiser Squadron, Second, Third and Sixth Cruiser Squadrons, First Light Cruiser Squadron and Second and Fourth Flotillas. These elements rendezvoused at 9.30am the next day to sweep south through the North Sea, with Beatty's battlecruisers considerably in the van.

The Harwich Force, with Tyrwhitt's three cruisers, the three carriers and eight destroyers, weighed on the morning of the 23rd, to advance into Heligoland Bight as in October and reach seaplane take-off position 24 hours later. But this time the carriers did not get even as far as they had previously, for during the night of the 23rd to the 24th an Admiralty signal was received cancelling the aerial portion of the operation. Conflicting reasons have been given. According to Jellicoe, 'it was thought that the enemy had a force present in the Bight, which would be too strong for our detached vessels,'[14] while Churchill states that 'in the weather prevailing the seaplanes could hardly get off the water'.[15]

But although the carriers and their escorting destroyers turned back, the purely surface portion of the operation proceeded. Shortly after the signal for cancellation of the air attack was received, Tyrwhitt was ordered by Jellicoe, under whose command the Harwich Force now came, to stand by and link up with the Second Cruiser Squadron at its daylight position of 54° 50′ north latitude, 7° 5′ east longitude. The combined squadrons then were to advance toward the island of Heligoland and try to lure any enemy forces found toward the main fleet. Tyrwhitt, with *Arethusa*, *Aurora* and *Undaunted*, plus the destroyer *Lennox*, which had gone astray from the carriers, complied, and during the morning the two cruiser squadrons approached to visual distance of Heligoland while to the north-west Beatty's battlecruisers advanced to 140 miles of the island with the Battle Fleet 40 miles behind them.

Smoke and what were thought to be destroyers were sighted behind the island, but the enemy refused to be enticed. The only visible countermeasures were taken by the Heligoland naval air base. Three of the six seaplanes stationed there were serviceable that day, and two of these took off after smoke from the British ships was seen. One had to turn back with engine and elevator trouble, but the second, a Friedrichshafen FF 19, attacked at 12.35pm a ship the airmen correctly identified as a *Bristol* class cruiser. All five bombs dropped missed the target, *Liverpool* of the Second Cruiser Squadron, although the aviators mistakenly claimed one hit.

While German seaplanes had skirmished with British submarines in the bight previously, this would appear to be the first aerial attack ever made on a British surface warship. Tyrwhitt, witnessing it from a distance, regretted the seaplane was out of range of *Arethusa*'s 'aerial guns'.[16] By this time it was apparent that the enticing action had failed. Tyrwhitt was detached to return to Harwich, and at 2pm the Battle Fleet turned to the north-west, ending the operation.

Cancellation of the aerial attack was again galling to Tyrwhitt, but this time he could hardly blame the air service. In retrospect, the decision seems ill-grounded. Churchill's explanation for it cannot be accepted; apparently he confused weather conditions of 24 November with those of 25 October. Far from being too difficult for seaplanes, the weather on the 24th appears to have been ideal – Jellicoe described that morning as 'fine and bright with high visibility'[17] and Tyrwhitt called it 'lovely, calm and clear'.[18] Certainly the German seaplanes had no trouble taking off.

The reason given by Jellicoe for the cancellation was almost certainly the real one. The Germans did indeed have a strong force in the bight – Vize Admiral Franz Hipper's battlecruisers of Scouting Group I, working-up a recently joined unit, *Derfflinger*,[19] and this fact was discovered by British electronic intelligence. But this squadron had returned to port by dawn of the 24th. It might have rushed back to sea if the carriers and their escorts had been spotted (although it did not do so in response to the British cruisers' appearance off Heligoland) but that would have been exactly the situation hoped for when the enticing action was planned.

Jellicoe's explanation reveals the fatal flaw in this planning – the fact that all elements of the Grand Fleet were too distant to protect the 'detached vessels' which as Tyrwhitt pointed out later were not equal to a single German battlecruiser in a daylight action.[20] The error in placing supporting forces too far away to permit them to give timely assistance would appear glaringly obvious, but it was to be repeated time and again during the war. It was in a sense the maritime equivalent of the British army's repeated error on the Western Front of failing to mass sufficient reserves to exploit temporary penetrations of the German lines. Fortunately for the Royal Navy, it was never required to pay the bloody penalty exacted from the army by faulty staff work.

CHAPTER 4

Plan Y

Planning for the next attempt began soon after the November failure. The first of the unsolved mysteries of the Cuxhaven Raid arises over the projected date for the new venture. According to Tyrwhitt's biographer, it was to take place a few days before Christmas, and its postponment to the 25th (much to the annoyance of the commodore's wife, for it upset her holiday plans) was caused by German intelligence getting wind of the scheme.[1] But Tyrwhitt's orders for the operation, dated 2 December, specifically set the sailing date as 24 December. Mrs Tyrwhitt's annoyance may well have been caused simply by the fact that a naval officer keeps secrets even from his nearest and dearest, but it is difficult to understand how the commodore could confidently date three weeks in advance an operation so dependent on the weather, especially considering the inadequacies of long-range weather forecasting in 1914. Adding to the mystery are the dates of other orders for the operation. Those of Keyes to his submarines (which, as will be detailed later, were now for the first time given a role in the venture) were issued on 7 December, but Sueter's orders for the aerial portion did not appear until 18 December and the instructions of the officer in tactical command of the seaplanes were not given until 21 December.

Meanwhile, in mid-December there occurred an event that would have an indirect, but definite, influence on the Cuxhaven Raid: Hipper's battlecruisers bombarded the coastal towns of Hartlepool, Whitby and Scarborough, escaping in a chase that involved the Harwich Force. This was actually an enticing move, intended to draw an inferior British force into action with the main body of the High Seas Fleet, which was supporting Hipper at a distance. But in Britain, this episode of 16 December, the first major attack on English soil since the Dutch wars of the seventeenth century, was a sensation, rousing a fury of indignation against Germany and recrimination against the Royal Navy for failing to prevent the bombardment or take revenge on its executioners.*

As a result of this uproar, on 21 December Beatty's battlecruiser force was ordered south to be based at Rosyth (on Scotland's Firth of Forth) where it would be better placed to cope with any future such German foray. We shall note later what effect this move had on the Cuxhaven Raid.

That same date (21 December) saw completion of plans and orders for the new sea-borne aerial attack. Basically, it was to be repetition of the November operation. The target of the seaplanes was again what was still called the Cuxhaven base, although now British intelligence had learned the base was not in the close vicinity of the city but believed it was to the south and about ten miles inland – a fairly accurate estimate. A report that the base now housed four Zeppelins, however, was incorrect.

As in November, it was thought that the attack might set the stage for a fleet action, so once more the Grand Fleet was to concentrate in the mid-North Sea, though again too distant to offer any support to the Harwich Force. But this time a new protective element was added by Admiralty planners. A line of Keyes' submarines was to be stationed south of Heligoland off the German coast with a two-fold mission: to attack enemy vessels that might sortie against the carriers and their escorts and to rescue airmen who might come down at sea, also ensuring destruction of ditched planes so they would not fall into German hands. Keyes, deeply concerned about the wide gap between the Harwich Force and its nearest big-gun support, felt keenly the responsibility this mission placed on his boats. He impressed on their officers that they must 'drive home their attacks, proceed to the assistance of seaplanes, or carry out any other service which might arise, regardless of all other considerations.'[2]

Sueter's orders for Plan Y, as the raid was designated (an apparently arbitrary code name) called for *Engadine*, *Riviera* and *Empress* each to carry her full complement of three seaplanes and each plane to carry three 20-pound bombs, 'it having been proved that one of these bombs will destroy a Zeppelin in a shed'[3] (an obvious reference to the destruction of *Z IX* in October). The airship shed was the target of priority, but if it could not be found or attacked the planes were to 'attack the enemy's ships or any positions of military importance.'[4]

*There had been no comparable outcry after a similar bombardment of the Yarmouth area on 3 November, for the German shells then had simply churned up water and sand, causing no damage or casualties.

In addition, subsidiary reconnaissance missions were assigned, to be undertaken after the bombing attempt. Planes from *Empress* were to 'count the ships' in Schillig Roads which was the enemy fleet's concentration point, north of Wilhelmshaven; those from *Engadine* were to perform the same mission at Wilhelmshaven itself, and *Riviera*'s three were to reconnoitre the eastern portion of the bight and shipping at the mouth of the Elbe River.

It is time to examine the aircraft to which these tasks were assigned. Three types were represented, all manufactured by the pioneering aviation firm of Short Brothers Ltd, prinicipal supplier of seaplanes to the Royal Navy since the first British seaplane had flown three years previously and whose association with maritime aircraft would continue for decades to come. The three, the Admiralty Type 74, the Folder, and the Admiralty Type 135, were basically similar: all were single-engined, two-seater biplanes with twin main floats and auxiliary floats under each lower wing-tip and under the tail.

The Type 74 was the oldest of the three designs, an improved version of the Royal Navy's first seaplane, the Short S 41 of 1912.

Table I

Distribution of Aircraft and Personnel on Carriers for Cuxhaven Raid

Aircraft number	Aircraft type	Carrier	Pilot and Observer
119	Folder	*Engadine*	Flight Cdr Robert P Ross None
120	Folder	*Engadine*	Flight Lt Arnold J Miley None
122	Folder	*Engadine*	Flight Cdr A B Gaskell None
135	135	*Riviera*	Flight Cdr Francis E T Hewlett None
136	135	*Riviera*	Flight Cdr Cecil F Kilner Lt Robert Erskine Childers
811	74	*Riviera*	Flight Lt Charles H K Edmonds None
812	74	*Empress*	Flight Lt Reginald J Bone Air Mechanic Waters
814	74	*Empress*	Flight Sub-Lt Vivian Gaskell Blackburn Chief Petty Officer James Bell
815	74	*Empress*	Flight Cdr Douglas A Oliver Chief Petty Officer Budds

All technical particulars of this plane have been lost over the years save the fact it was powered by a 100-horsepower Gnome rotary engine.* Several Type 74s were in RNAS service at the start of the war, but the exact number is not known. Four were to be embarked on the Cuxhaven Raid, three of them aboard *Empress*. (See Table I for distribution of aircraft among the carriers.)

The next most numerous type embarked was the Folder; three were used. This plane took its name from the feature it introduced into shipboard aviation, namely the folding wing, patented in 1913 by Short Brothers under the strong encouragement of Churchill. This permitted its wings to be swung back parallel to the fuselage, reducing their 67-foot span to no more than 12 feet, greatly simplifying shipboard carriage. The advantage of this feature had been amply demonstrated in 1913 when an earlier, shorter-span version of the Folder was successfully operated by the cruiser *Hermes*. The later versions, of the type used in the Cuxhaven Raid, were powered by 160-horsepower Gnome rotaries, had a maximum speed of 78mph and a fully loaded weight of 3040 pounds. The Folder was designed to be a torpedo plane, although it was never used as such, and the RNAS had at least eight of the type at the outbreak of war.

The Type 135, ordered by the navy in September 1913, was a still improved version of the Folder, including the folding wing feature. Only two were constructed, No 135, powered by a 135-horsepower Salmson single-row radial engine, and No 136, with a 200-horsepower twin-row Salmson (the Salmson was called the Canton-Unné by the RNAS). Somewhat smaller than the Folder, with a wing-span of 54 feet 6 inches, it had a higher loaded weight (3700 pounds) and was generally a superior aircraft both in the air and on water. The higher-powered No 136, which was not delivered until after war began, was for a brief period probably the finest maritime aircraft of its time. It survived the Cuxhaven Raid to render valuable service at the Dardanelles in early 1915.[5] It was soon eclipsed, however, by another seaplane under development in late 1914, the Short Admiralty Type 184.

Altogether, the nine aircraft destined for the Cuxhaven Raid

---

*The rotary engine, long vanished from the aviation scene, was used extensively before, during and for a short time after World War I. Its unique feature was that the entire engine rotated along with the propeller around a fixed crankcase. It was long favoured because of its light weight (its air cooling eliminated the need for a radiator system) and consequent high ratio of horsepower to weight. But it was mechanically complex, necessitating constant maintenance and having a short life even with that maintenance; required considerable skill to operate, and had a high rate of fuel and oil consumption.

The target of the Cuxhaven Raid, the twin revolving airship hangar at Nordholz as it looked later in the war, probably during the winter of 1917-18. Its 1914 appearance has been somewhat altered by the addition of 'Busen' protruberances to accommodate the longer, later airships. *By courtesy of Dr Douglas H Robinson*

were as good as any other seaplanes in the world in 1914, and superior to many. But it was pure chance that resulted in their selection for the raid – they were chosen merely because they were available. They had no formal organization or designation but were arbitrarily assigned, along with their pilots and mechanics, to the various carriers (although once assigned, the attachment was fairly permanent). The planes were embarked only for specific missions, otherwise remaining ashore, where shelter was more secure and maintenance easier to carry out.

Ad hoc as this formation was, it did have a commanding officer, Squadron Commander Cecil J L'Estrange Malone, one of the most interesting personalities of the Cuxhaven Raid. Malone wore three hats: he was in tactical command of the seaplanes, the man who had to arrange all the practical matters of technical preparation; he was captain of *Engadine*; and he was commanding officer of all three carriers at sea. These were weighty responsibilities for a young officer who, as Keyes notes, had been given them 'over the heads of many seniors'.[6] But belying his years and his rank, Malone was one of the great pioneers of naval aviation. His air service pre-dated formation of the RNAS, he had been the second man in the world (after Samson) to fly an aeroplane from a moving ship (and the third in the world to take off from a ship at all), and was one of the officers responsible for the genesis of the British torpedo plane. Malone was an early and strong advocate of the offensive use of aircraft in naval warfare, and especially of the torpedo plane. In 1915 he finally had a chance to put his theories into practice when, as captain of the seaplane carrier *Ben-my-Chree* at the Dardanelles, he launched the world's first torpedo plane attacks.* His preparation of the Cuxhaven Raid can stand as a model of thoroughness and efficiency.

Malone's two principal subordinates, Lieutenant E D M Robertson, captain of *Riviera*, and Lieutenant Frederick W Bowhill, skipper of *Empress*,** were also RNAS officers. It was one of the strengths of early British naval aviation that nearly all Royal Navy aviation vessels were captained by air service officers until formation of the Royal Air Force in 1918. This policy seems to have evolved informally rather than being the result of administrative decision. Whatever the reason for the policy, it proved an excellent one, resulting in maximum co-ordination and integration of surface and aerial elements by officers thoroughly familiar with both. This situation ended in 1918, forbidden by the legislation that created the RAF. By contrast, legislation passed in the United States in 1926 mandated that aviation vessels could be commanded *only* by qualified naval aviators or naval air observers. This difference in policy does much to explain the disparity in progress between American and British shipboard air arms during the interwar period.

Malone was assisted in his preparations by a figure of magnetic interest, destined within a few years for lasting world fame – Royal Navy Volunteer Reserve Lieutenant Robert Erskine Chil-

---

* Malone later commanded the four-carrier Egypt and East Indies Seaplane Squadron, whose vessels and aircraft operated in the eastern Mediterranean and Red Sea, and then became second-in-command of this squadron under Samson. The Armistice found him a lieutenant colonel in the Royal Air Force. Entering Parliament after the war, he became too strong a partisan of the Soviet government during the period of British intervention in the Russian civil war and in 1920 he was sentenced to six months in prison under the Defence of the Realm Act.

** Bowhill was unique among prewar naval aviators (and later among Royal Air Force marshals) in having earned a master's certificate under sail before joining the navy. He commanded the air contingent of the British naval force in the Caspian Sea just after World War I. Achieving a knighthood and rising to the rank of Air Chief Marshal, he had a distinguished later career including command of the RAF Coastal Command (1937-41), Ferry Command and Transport Command.

ders (better known simply as Erskine Childers), soldier, novelist, historian, civil servant, gun-runner, yachtsman, parliamentarian, revolutionist, guerrilla, hero and martyr of Irish independence, and father of the late fourth president of the Irish Republic.

Childers had reported for duty at the Felixstowe Naval Air Station on 18 August.[7] The fact that less than a month earlier he and his American-born wife had been smuggling German rifles and ammunition to Ireland aboard his yacht *Asgard* had not prevented his volunteering to fight again for the country he had served as an artilleryman in the Boer War. Although 44 years old in 1914, nearly twice the age of many of his air service compatriots, Childers was tough and hardy from a strenuous life, as fit for service as any younger man. But he was far from being merely one more willing hand; his value, and the reason his services were accepted enthusiastically by a pleased Admiralty, resided in his almost unique knowledge of German coastal waters.

Short Folder No 119, one of the three aircraft of its type embarked on HMS *Engadine* for the Cuxhaven Raid and flown by Robert P Ross. *Fleet Air Arm Museum*

To appreciate how precious this knowledge was to planning the Cuxhaven Raid, it is necessary to examine Germany's North Sea coast, in 1914 stretching no more than 200 miles between the Danish and Dutch borders. It was the approximately 70-mile western portion of this coast that concerned the Royal Navy, for it was there the German fleet based in ports and anchorages, clustered about the estuaries of four rivers: the Ems, Jade, Weser and Elbe.

The westernmost river, the Ems, separating Germany and Holland, has Emden as its principal port. Only light craft and

Short Admiralty Type 74 seaplane, the original No 74 itself. Four aircraft of this type were embarked for the Cuxhaven Raid. *Fleet Air Arm Museum*

small cruisers were stationed there in 1914, although it was an important submarine base. The easternmost river, the Elbe, is the gateway to the great port of Hamburg, and on it lies Brunsbüttel, western entrance to the Kiel Canal. The next river to the west, the Weser, leads to Bremerhaven and Bremen. Between the Weser and the Elbe is a blunt, low-lying semi-peninsula, dyked in many areas, near the tip of which is located Cuxhaven. Up the Elbe, between Cuxhaven and Brunsbüttel, was one of the High Seas Fleet's major anchorages, off Altenbruch.

The final river is the Jade, flowing from landlocked Jade Bay to converge with the Weser. On the north-west side of Jade Bay lay Wilhelmshaven, a fishing village that had grown with the rise of the Imperial Navy to become that navy's principal port, a bustling city with dockyards, warehouses, quays, workshops, factories, and magazines – all the industrial facilities required by a great and growing fleet. The Jade, although broad, was tortuous to navigate, littered with shifting sandbanks, subject to silting of the passages that had to be dredged for the battleships and requiring careful maintenance of channel-marking buoys and lights. Even with these aids, the passage of deep-draught ships was governed by tides. Ten miles out, however, the waters widened to become Schillig Roads, the main fleet anchorage. Here the fleet would rendezvous preparatory to sorties, capital ships coming from Jade Bay, cruisers from the Weser, and destroyers from the Elbe.

The entrance to all these fleet bases and concentration points were heavily fortified, dotted with low-lying emplacements for guns of all calibres. Out in the bight, 40 miles from Cuxhaven and 48 miles from Wilhelmshaven, lies the island of Heligoland, also well fortified in 1914. Its harbour had insufficient depth of water to accommodate large vessels but could be used by light craft and small cruisers, and it was the site of one of the Imperial Navy's first prewar seaplane stations.

A few miles north and slightly west of Schillig Roads is Wangeroog, easternmost of the German (or East) Frisian Islands. There are six other main islands in the approximately 50-mile German portion of this chain. They are from east to west: Spiekeroog, Langeoog, Baltrum, Norderney, Juist and Borkum, the latter lying off the mouth of the Ems. The waters around these islands, and the dune-covered East Friesland coast off which they lie, are an intricate maze of shallow tidal channels and inlets, a labyrinth of sandflats, great expanses of which are totally exposed at low tide.

Childers, who had a lifelong love of sailing, had spent years exploring this watery wilderness between the Elbe and Borkum, navigating a series of small boats through it, sometimes single-handed, sometimes with a crew consisting of his brother, a friend or two, or his wife. These voyages had started before the turn of the century, and continued almost annually during the decade before the war. The cruises had taken him as far afield as Norway and the Baltic, but the Frisian coast and the German estuaries were his favourite waters.

Childers made use of this special knowledge in his enormously successful novel of 1903, *The Riddle of the Sands*, his only piece of fiction. Considered by many critics to be the direct ancestor of the spy-thriller/mystery genre so popular in recent decades, this story of two holidaying seafarers' discovery of a German plot to invade Britain remains as gripping and readable today as it was three-quarters of a century ago.*

Since the Cuxhaven Raid was to take the British seaplanes over precisely this area known so well to Childers (from the Elbe to Norderney) his role in the raid's preparation was vital. Malone had high praise for

---

* One of Childers' sailing companions, who became an intimate friend and who took part in the gun-running of July 1914, was Gordon S Shephard, a young army officer and equally avid sailor. In 1912 Shephard transferred to the Royal Flying Corps and by the time he was killed in an accidental crash in 1918 had risen to brigadier general – at the age of 32 the youngest of his rank. Shephard made many cruises of his own along the German coast, actually spying upon and photographing its fortifications, apparently at the unofficial behest of the British War Office and Admiralty. At one point in 1911 his actions became so suspicious that he had and a companion were detained and questioned by the German police. These activities later gave rise to the story that the plot of *The Riddle of the Sands* was based on one of Shephard's spying voyages – completely untrue, since Shephard did not begin his nautical espionage before making Childers' acquaintance in 1909, six years after publication of the novel.

the valuable assistance rendered by Lieutenant Erskine Childers RNVR, whose knowledge and experience connected with the navigation of the German coast proved invaluable in instructing the pilots,

and

the energy expended by him in preparing charts and collecting topographical data.[8]

This praise was echoed by Robertson, captain of *Riviera*, from which, as we shall see, Childers flew in a real-life adventure far more thrilling and dangerous than his fictional one: 'His knowledge of the German coast and landmarks, which has been imparted as far as possible to the pilots, has proved *invaluable* to them.'[9] And 'invaluable' recurs as the adjective chosen by Keyes in his tribute to Childers' contribution.[10]

Although Childers' latest biographer states he was to lead the seaplanes as as a sort of chief observer, that implies a kind of organized formation flying almost unheard of then in the Royal Naval Air Service. RNAS aircraft *had* appeared in formation during the Spithead Fleet Review in July, having specially practised for this at Eastchurch, but formation flying under service conditions was still considered too difficult and did not appear to have much value anyhow. It was not adopted by the Royal Flying Corps until January 1916.[11] While Plan Y was not specific on the point, it may be assumed that individual seaplanes were to find their way to their target at the initiative of each pilot.

Under the plan, the planes were to take off from a point north-east of Heligoland island and fly south-west to make a landfall in the vicinity of Cuxhaven, proceeding to seek out and attack the airship base. After that, they were to carry out, if possible, the reconnaissance missions described earlier. The broad observations noted by Sueter were broken down into more specific points of information desired in a list prepared by the Admiralty and given to the airmen by Malone in his orders of 21 December. It was sought to learn whether the Elbe lightvessels were still in place, if a swept channel led through a minefield outside the Jade and if so whether its buoys could be seen, the exact anchorages of ships in Schillig Roads, the number and classes of vessels at Wilhelmshaven, the location of a boom believed to be defending Schillig Roads, and finally, 'If there are any targets for ships in Schilling [Schillig] Roads to fire at, where are they? – and what are they like?'[12] But it was emphasized that desirable as this information was, it was not to be obtained 'to the detriment of the main objective.'[13]

After the attack and the reconnaissances, the planes were to turn westward and follow the Frisian Island chain to Norderney. At the Norderney Gat (gap), the channel between that island and Juist (the next to the west) they were to turn and fly a north (magnetic) course to rejoin the carriers, which with their escorts would have reached a point 20 miles north of Norderney.

The aerial operation was to be preceded and accompanied by carefully synchronized movements by the surface and sub-surface units based at Harwich, and an even more extensive nautical ballet by the Grand Fleet far to the north. At Harwich, the submarines, because of their slow surface and even slower submerged speeds, were first off the mark. Under the orders given by Keyes, they were to sail in pairs during the night of 23 to 24 December to be in position by dawn of 25 December: *E 6* and *E 15* at 9pm on the 23rd, followed at intervals by *E 12* and *E 13*, *D 6* and *E 11*, *D 8* and *D 7*; and finally, at 3am on the 24th, *S 1* and *E 10*. An eleventh boat, *E 7*, was already on station south of Heligoland between the entrances of the Weser and the Jade and was to remain there during the raid.

Friedrichshafen FF 19s, No 25 and No 26 at Heligoland. No 25, flying from the island's air station, took part in attacks on British ships during the Cuxhaven Raid and was so badly damaged by British gunfire that it became a total loss. *Author's collection*

55

The first four boats were to take positions between 54° 23′ north latitude, 8° 2′ east longitude and 54° 0′ north latitude, 7° 0′ east longitude, and generally patrol along a line between those positions from 6am to noon, on the look-out for strayed seaplanes. *E 6*, however, was given the special mission of caring for planes that might have failed to take off, and then cruising in the vicinity of Heligoland until nightfall.

Of the other submarines, *E 11* was to take up position north of the Norderney lighthouse, *D 6* off the Norderney Gat, *D 8* off central Juist, *D 7* at the east end of Borkum, and *S 1* and *E 10* at the western and eastern ends, respectively, of the Ems channels that curve around Borkum. *D 6* and *D 8* were to surface at 9am 'to give the seaplanes a mark and assist them if necessary'[14] and proceed northward 30 minutes later; *D 7* was to turn east at 9am and cruise northward of the Norderney Gat; and *E 11* was to observe the inshore channel between the Ems and the Jade.

Lurcher, with Keyes aboard, and *Firedrake* were to leave Harwich at 6am on the 24th and stand off the Norderney Gat 'to give warning to the squadron if the enemy approaches from the Ems or through the swept channel from the eastward.'[15]

The three carriers, with *Arethusa*, *Undaunted* and eight destroyers of the Third Flotilla, were to sail at 5am on 24 December, to reach the seaplane launching point, 54° 27′ north latitude, 8° 00′ east longitude, by 6am on the 25th. 'It is estimated', Tyrwhitt wrote, 'that it will be sufficiently light to fly at about 7am if the morning is fine.'[16] Two hours before the launching point was reached, *Undaunted* was to reduce speed to 13 knots and lag behind to 'form a guard in case of attack from the north,'[17] keeping at least three miles from the seaplane take-off position. As soon as the planes were in the air, the surface force, rejoined by *Undaunted*, was to proceed south by 'a circuitous route' to the recovery position north of Norderney.

For the final element in the operation, *Fearless* and eight destroyers of the First Flotilla, under command of Captain W F Blunt, were to leave Harwich at 10am on the 24th, to reach 54° 2′ north latitude, 6° 3′ east longitude, by 5.30am the next day. This squadron was to cruise in that vicinity, 'taking care to keep out of sight of land,'[18] until 8am, when it was to proceed at high speed for a rendezvous with Tyrwhitt to give support 'in the event of an attack while picking up the seaplanes.'[19]

A three-hour time limit was laid down for return and recovery of the planes; at the end of that period the entire surface force was to retire westward and then alter course for home. A strong thread of concern over safe recovery of the aviators runs through

Short No 135, the seaplane flown by Francis E T Hewlett in the Cuxhaven Raid, afloat with wings folded, possibly alongside HMS *Riviera*. The men perched on the floats are probably RNAS mechanics. *By courtesy of Dr Arthur Hewlett, via Michael B Goodall*

Tyrwhitt's and Keyes' orders. It was emphasized that this should take priority unless vessels were actually engaged with the enemy, and should be done on individual initiative without the need for special orders from the flagship or the carriers.

While rescue of the airmen was the main concern, considerable attention was paid to preserving the seaplanes. Destruction of the aircraft was, of course, preferable to their abandonment to the enemy, but 'this measure is not to be resorted to unless it is obvious that we are likely to be overpowered by a superior force.'[20] Destroyers were to go to the aid of planes unable to reach the carriers, and Tyrwhitt instructed their captains to use great care and slow speed in approaching a plane on the water, as the effect of the ship's wash could be 'disastrous'. Nor were destroyers to attempt towing seaplanes at more than ten knots. To enable the commodore 'to see at a glance how many pilots are accounted for,' a destroyer picking up an airman was to hoist a black ball at its yardarm.

If salvage of a plane seemed impossible, destroyers and

submarines were to make every effort to recover its engine – a logical order, since engines were the most valuable components of the planes, and in shorter supply than airframes in 1914.[21] Destroyers were instructed to have their torpedo davits rigged for this possibility.

Tyrwhitt was grimly aware that his squadron might well encounter the 'superior force' of which he wrote. In this case, he ordered, the carriers were to steam southward at highest possible speed toward the Dutch island of Terschelling, then proceed to 'the nearest [British] port with all dispatch, separating if chased.'[22] The destroyers meanwhile were to take over the mission of pilot rescue, and destroy rather than attempt to save the seaplanes.

Whatever the likelihood of a surface action, all hands seemed convinced that attack by German aircraft was a near certainty.[25] Since this opened up the probability of British and German seaplanes being over the ships at the same time, Tyrwhitt and Keyes went to pains, including sketches in their orders, to impress on their subordinates the British aerial recognition symbols: red circles enclosing a white centre on upper wing surfaces, supplemented by Union Jacks on lower wings.*

The presence of German submarines also was considered inevitable, and since there was little difference in appearance between a U-boat and an E-boat, an identification device was adopted to help the British fliers distinguish friend from foe. All the British submarines taking part in the operation were to have a broad red and white checkered stripe painted round their conning towers. This marking was, as we shall see later, to prove valuable to at least one aviator.

Whether on the basis of the date scheduled by Tyrwhitt or because of a forecast of favourable weather for Christmas Day (it does not seem possible to determine which), Plan Y began to go into effect on 23 December. The seaplanes and their personnel were embarked on the carriers that evening, and during the night the submarines slipped as ordered, the last pair leaving their berths before dawn on 24 December. By 4.45am that day the carriers, as ordered by Malone, had raised steam for 15 knots and

---

* The Union Jack was the first insignia of British military and naval aircraft, but planes bearing it were often fired upon by friendly forces because at a distance it could resemble a German cross. Consequently, it was abandoned by the Royal Flying Corps after October, 1914, replaced by the classic blue, white and red roundel. The Royal Naval Air Service, however, adopted instead the red circle with white centre and continued to use this device, along with the Union Jack, until well into 1915, when the RFC-style roundel was finally substituted.

proceeded to sea: *Engadine* was followed by *Riviera* and *Empress*, to join *Arethusa*, *Undaunted* and eight destroyers – the 'L' class vessels *Lawford*, *Lennox*, *Leonidas*, *Lookout*, *Lydiard* and *Lysander*, and two newer ones of the 'M' class, *Miranda* (leader of the destroyer unit) and *Minos*. At 5am, exactly on schedule, the squadron began to shape course for the bight. Despite the strong indication of impending action given by the embarkation of the seaplanes the previous evening, the operation had been kept secret so well that several stewards and messmen who had gone ashore to buy ingredients for their ships' Christmas dinners were stranded on the quayside with their delicacies.[24]

Five hours later, *Fearless* and eight 'I' class destroyers sailed in Tyrwhitt's wake. The Cuxhaven Raid was under way.

Folder No 120 photographed at Westgate. *By courtesy of J M Bruce via G S Leslie*

Robert P Ross photographed in 1916. He was pilot of Folder No 119, embarked from HMS *Engadine*. *Fleet Air Arm Museum*

CHAPTER 5

It Was a Star

The Harwich Force and its carriers, although the spearhead of the raid, constituted only the tip of the iceberg in a complex assemblage of Royal Navy strength. From the evening of 24 December through the morning of the next day, elements of the Grand Fleet, more than 100 ships in all, steamed from their various bases for a concentration in the mid-North Sea. Through the Pentland Firth from gunnery practice north of the Hebrides came the Second and Fourth Battle Squadrons with Jellicoe's flagship, *Iron Duke*. From Scapa Flow steamed the First Battle Squadron, Sixth Cruiser Squadron and Second Flotilla. Rosyth contributed the Third Battle Squadron (the 'Wobbly Eight' *King Edward VII* class pre-dreadnoughts), First Battle Cruiser Squadron, Third Cruiser Squadron and First Light Cruiser Squadron. Setting sail from Cromarty were the the First and Second Cruiser Squadrons and the Fourth Flotilla.[1]

Altogether, the vessels employed to carry out the aerial attack and give it direct or indirect support numbered perhaps as many as 150, ranging from minesweeping trawlers to super-dreadnoughts. The ultimate purpose of this armada was to deliver to the German mainland exactly 81½ pounds of explosive. This figure was the combined weight of the bursting charges in the 27 bombs to be carried by the seaplanes and weighing 3½ pounds less than the similar charge in only one of the 13.5-inch common shells in the *Iron Duke*'s magazines. But just one of the seaplanes' bombs could accomplish what a broadside from the entire Grand Fleet could not. For the first time in the history of naval warfare, shipboard aircraft were to be the sole striking arm of a fleet.

Soon after leaving harbour the embryonic carrier task force took up the cruising formation Tyrwhitt had ordered for the daylight hours. It was a tight and compact disposition: ahead of *Arethusa*, Tyrwhitt's flagship, was a fan-like anti-submarine screen of four

61

destroyers, spread out at respective distances of 700, 600, 600 and 700 yards off the cruiser's bows. *Engadine* and *Riviera* followed *Arethusa* in column, with intervals of 1½ cables (approximately 300 yards) between ships. A mile behind *Riviera* steamed *Undaunted*, preceded by four destroyers disposed identically to those screening *Arethusa* and followed at 1½ cables by *Empress*. The reason for splitting the carriers into two groups is not clear, but it may have been to separate *Empress* from her faster compatriots in case high-speed manoeuvring became necessary. However, all the carriers were to close and function together during seaplane launching.

The daylight hours passed uneventfully for the force. Malone wrote:

> The weather throughout the whole passage across was most propitious, and at 2pm everything was got ready to enable seaplanes to be hoisted out on arrival.[2]

For the RNAS mechanics, this meant removing the pins securing the wings of the folding-wing planes and lashing them closed with lines that could be removed in a trice, reeving steadying lines to the floats and wing tips, and preparing the lines that would hoist the planes onto the water. Each plane was to be fuelled for a flight of three hours duration. This was less than the maximum amount of fuel that could be carried, but reduced the weight that had to be lifted from the water, always a big consideration in operating seaplanes in 1914. Moreover, three hours appeared to be long enough to accomplish the raid's objective, while at the same time the maximum period the weak surface force could risk its presence deep inside waters controlled by the second most powerful navy in the world. As it turned out, the three-hour limit was a miscalculation, although the reason could not have been known in advance. One officer, however, did mistrust the calculation – *Riviera*'s Robertson, who insisted his pilots carry fuel for four hours. 'I think,' he wrote later, 'that although decreasing the lift, events justified the decision.'[3] As we shall see, events did indeed.

The same consideration of weight to be lifted from water seems responsible for the order that each plane was to carry only three bombs, a load lighter than maximum capacity. These pear-shaped missiles were slung on racks on the centre sections of the planes between the main floats and were released from the cockpit by Bowden wire. Surviving documents do not mention the kind of bombsight used, but it could have been the so-called lever type, a hand-held device developed during prewar and early war days.[4]

The bombs themselves had been devised for the RNAS in 1913 by F Martin Hale, a well-known expert in explosives and ballistics who was responsible for several innovations in ordnance; they were manufactured by the Cotton Powder Company of Faversham, Kent. The 20-pound Hales bombs, as they were known, actually weighed 18½ pounds including a 4½-pound bursting charge of amatol, a mixture of TNT and ammonium nitrate. They were armed by a fusing mechanism activated by a small propeller behind the tail fins that began to revolve when the missile was dropped.[5]

While their mechanics were readying the seaplanes, the pilots aboard the carriers were preparing to outfit themselves with the considerable amount of equipment Malone specified they should carry on the raid: a revolver with six packets of ammunition, a flare pistol with six cartridges, a lifebelt, two flashlights ('electric torch lamps'), a box of matches, a knife, maps and charts, provisions for 48 hours, first aid dressings, as well as a long list of tools – 'King dicks, pliers, Jet spanner, ignition wire, rubber tubing, tape, copper drift hammer, screwdriver, HT wire, special tools and spare plugs, etc. as available.[6] Apart from the bombs, the pilots' pistols were the only armament carried in the seaplanes, although Flight Sub-lieutenant Vivian Gaskell Blackburn, pilot of Short 74 No 184 on *Riviera*, indicates he and his observer also lugged along a rifle.[7]

At 5pm, as dusk began to fall and the Harwich Force prepared for the most dangerous portion of its voyage, the night passage through the bight, the destroyers moved to the positions ordered by Tyrwhitt for the dark hours, abeam of *Arethusa* and *Undaunted* at six cables distance.

Meanwhile, back on home soil, a harbinger of the future went unknown to the men of the Harwich Force. A Zanonia-winged Gotha Taube from the German naval air unit at Mariakerke in Belgium, flown by Leutenant Karl Caspar, dropped a single bomb at Dover.[8] This missile, which exploded in a garden near Dover Castle and did no more damage than shattering a few windows, was the first of thousands that would rain on Britain during two wars.*

The tense hours of darkness remained uneventful as the Harwich Force bored deeper into the bight, showing no lights and keeping radio silence. The weather stayed as good as forecast – described as 'propitious' by Malone, with a calm sea and clear

* Three days earlier another German plane had tried to bomb Dover but failed, its two bombs falling into the harbour.

HMS *Ben-my-Chree*, typical of the seaplane carriers used in the Raid. A Sopwith Schneider seaplane is being transferred from the decks of HMS/M *E 7*. *Fleet Air Arm Museum*.

skies, although toward morning a light fog appeared to land-ward. At 4am, according to Tyrwhitt's first report on the operation, the squadron reached 51° 52' north latitude, 7° 1' east longitude, the point the commodore had designated as Position I, where *Undaunted* was to reduce speed.

Some time between then and 4.30am a crisis occurred when the British squadron encountered some small craft that Tyrwhitt later judged to be four trawlers of the German patrol lines.[9] Their sighting was shortly followed by a burst of low-power radio clatter that was assumed on *Arethusa*'s bridge to be a contact report beamed to Heligoland or the mainland. Within the next 30 minutes, 17 more German radio messages were overheard in the flagship's wireless room, all believed to be prefaced with what was thought an 'urgent' call sign.

This incident apparently brought Tyrwhitt as close to a *crise de nerfs* as that doughty seaman-warrior ever came. It seemed certain the Harwich Force had been discovered by the enemy, with still at least 90 minutes of steaming to go before the seaplane launching point was reached. To proceed, therefore, could be to sail into disaster. But it was unbearably galling to consider retreat when the ships had come so far and when, finally, after the earlier disappointments, all conditions appeared ideal for the air attack. The commodore had to make an agonizing decision and, he wrote later, 'I very nearly made up my mind to retire altogether before it was too late.'[10]

It was about this time, while Tyrwhitt was struggling to decide what to do, that, unknown then to anyone, the British sustained their first (although non-fatal) casuality of the operation. Sub-marine *S 1*, smallest and shortest-ranged of the Harwich flotilla, [11] had reached her station off the western channel of the Ems and was diving to await daybreak when she struck an underwater obstacle. The shock jolted off her detachable keel and she shot to the surface. Unable to resubmerge, she turned homeward.[11]

While *S 1* was limping west. Tyrwhitt reached his decision, aided by what appeared at first a threat. It was a light, low on the horizon dead ahead, slowly rising higher and growing steadily brighter. At first it was taken on *Arethusa*'s bridge to be 'a fire balloon or a Zeppelin with some extraordinary searchlight.'[13] Then the navigation officer, Lieutenant (later Vice Admiral) B C Watson, pointed out to the commodore that it was, after all, Christmas morning, and the light shone from the east. To a man of Tyrwhitt's bedrock Christian faith, that remark was enough. It was soon realized that the mystery light was the planet Venus, its intensity magnified by the light fog. But to Tyrwhitt 'it was a star, and I am … sure it was sent to cheer us up![14] There would be no turning back.

The British squadron reached the seaplane launching point, designated Position II by Tyrwhitt, almost on the dot of 6am, exactly on schedule. The location was about 12 miles north-east of Heligoland, well within visual distance of the island. Position II had been pin-pointed as 54° 27′ north latitude, 8° 00′ east longitude, but actually the ships hove slightly north of this exact spot – a difference so slight as to be inconsequential.

Upon receiving the 'stop' signal from *Arethusa*, the vessels moved in accordance with pre-given orders, without the need for further signals, into assigned positions for the take-off operation. The carriers closed up to line abreast, *Empress* to port of *Engadine*, *Riviera* to starboard. The destroyers stood off at six cable lengths on each flank, four to port, four to starboard, as an anti-submarine screen. They kept up a moving patrol but speed was restricted to 12 knots to avoid creating wakes that could damage the seaplanes. *Undaunted* had already dropped behind to her rearguard position; *Arethusa*'s location during this part of the operation is unrecorded.

As soon as the carriers had stopped their engines, Malone, by megaphone, ordered *Empress* and *Riviera* to join *Engadine* in hoisting out planes. 'This evolution was performed quickly and without any hitch.'[15] The speed is indicated by Bowhill, who recorded that *Empress* got her planes on the water in five minutes, six minutes and eight minutes, respectively.[16] By 6.30am or shortly after, all nine Shorts were bobbing on the water and their mechanics, working from precarious perches on the main floats, were starting to unfold wings of the Folders and the Type 135s and preparing engines to turn over.

In the absence as yet of a trained corps of RNAS observers, it was customary for pilots to take a mechanic or other enlisted aircraft technician along on flights. On this morning, Malone's report reveals, the pilots were given a choice in the matter. (The case of Childers, the only non-pilot officer to fly that day, was an exception; because of his specialized knowledge there was no question of his remaining behind.) Only the three pilots of *Empress* chose to fill the second cockpit; the mechanics from those planes 'whose pilots did not wish to carry passengers'[17] were returned to the carriers by small boat.

The reasoning of the pilots who chose to fly alone is easy enough to surmise. In those early days of aerial warfare, when bombs were sighted and released by the pilot alone, the presence of a second man in the plane could do nothing useful to assist in the primary offensive mission, the attack on the airship base, and his presence would simply add more weight to be lifted from water. An extra pair of eyes could be helpful in carrying out the requested reconnaissances, but these, it had been stressed, were strictly secondary to the bombing attack – and even this subsidiary task might not be aided much by an enlisted man with little or no training or experience in aerial observation and warship identification. But why some pilots chose to take a companion that day and others did not remains a mystery of the Cuxhaven Raid. Only one who was there that morning in the North Sea is qualified to judge.

Dawn broke over the cluster of ships and planes to reveal, as Tyrwhitt described it, 'weather conditions ... perfect for flying, light airs from the eastward, sea calm, but ... bitterly cold.'[18] Perfect for flying, perhaps, but only if the planes could get into the air. The bitter cold aggravated the always temperamental business of starting engines, which coughed, sputtered, and fell silent as the mechanics struggled again and again to get them to kick over. The engine of one *Riviera* plane, Type 74 No 811, of Flight Lieutenant Charles H K Edmonds, faltered after the mechanics had already been taken off. These two brave men, Ernest J Wright, Chief Petty Officer Engineer Mechanic, and George A Kent, Air Mechanic First Grade, jumped from their gig and swam back through the bone-chilling water to nurse the Gnome into life again – an act that drew high commendation from Edmonds, Malone and Robertson.

At 6.54am Malone judged it was light enough for flying and hoisted the preparatory signal, two black balls on *Engadine*'s fore topmast, alerting pilots to stand by for take-off in five minutes. His orders had specified that the three older and slower planes, the Folders, would take off first, followed five minutes later by the higher-powered Shorts. But when at 6.59am the lower black ball was lowered to signal the Folders to get underway, not one, because of engine difficulties, was able to start. One of them, No 122, piloted by Flight Commander A B Gaskell, never did get into the air, whether due to engine failure or inability to 'unstick' from the water is not clear. Eventually the plane was hoisted back aboard *Engadine*.

Malone decided to risk an additional five-minute delay in ordering the second wave of planes off, until 7.09am. By this time some pilots apparently were ignoring his signals, for their reports state that Nos 184 and 815 from *Empress* were airborne at 7.00am and 7.05am respectively. Flight Commander Francis E T Hewlett in *Riviera*'s No 135 seems to have jumped the gun altogether, or confused his times, for he reported taking off at 6.56am.

Four more planes, after overcoming engine problems, got into the air at 7.10am: Nos 119 and 120 from *Engadine* and Nos 811 and 136 from *Riviera*. Two which had suffered complete engine failure

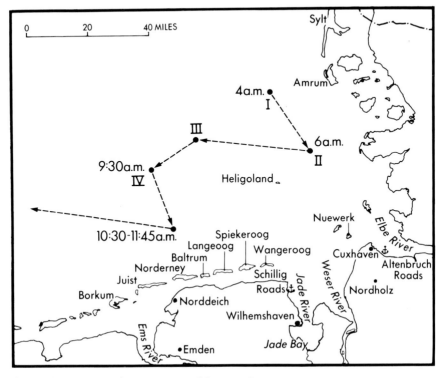

Approximate general courses (roughly to scale) steered by the Harwich carriers and their escorts during the Cuxhaven Raid. Roman numerals indicate positions of major pre-ordered course changes. The British seaplanes took off from Position II. Zeppelin *L 6* attacked *Empress* between Positions III and IV. *Map by Bruce Krefting based on* Arethusa's *course as shown in Admiralty Chart No 2182ᵃ, 26 January 1915, Public Record Office*

remained on the water, *Engadine*'s No 122 and *Riviera*'s No 812, which had suffered complete engine failture, with Flight Lieutenant Reginald J Bone and with Air Mechanic Waters.

Malone had planned a 15-minute limit for all planes to get airborne after his second take-off signal, but 'owing to the fact that extra time had been given and that smoke was visible from the direction of Heligoland, I hoisted the negative after 13 minutes' interval at 7.22am,'[19] shaving two minutes off the scheduled leeway. The two planes unable to take off were hoisted back aboard their carriers by 7.28am.

The take-offs had not been as simple as they might sound. The light wind and calm sea had forced long take-off runs[20]; some may have taken up to four minutes, resulting in a heavy use of fuel.

Already, before the Cuxhaven Raid was minutes old, the deceptively favourable weather had, by cheating the British of time and gasoline, proved an enemy. Now, as the seven planes winged their way south-east and the sun rose higher, a portent of how great an enemy the weather could be was detected. For while visibility to seaward remained unlimited, a faint haze was seen toward the German mainland, noticeable even to Keyes aboard *Lurcher* far to the westward. It was the first hint of what would be the most important factor in frustrating history's first carrier strike.

Friday, 25 December 1914: in far-off Flanders, British and German infantrymen would stage an impromptu, unsanctioned Christmas armistice, emerging from the sodden trenches that snaked through the battered Belgian countryside to fraternize awkwardly in blood-soaked no-man's-land and exchange meagre gifts of food and tobacco. But here, in the bone-chilling cold of the North Sea and along the frost-coated German coast, there would be no truce.

Folder No 120, flown by Arnold J Miley in the raid. He found 'no [airship] sheds and no fortified places worth attacking.' *By courtesy of J M Bruce via G S Leslie*

CHAPTER 6

A Major Attack ... Was to Be Expected

C hristmas Day was a holiday dear to the hearts of German sailors. Little Christmas trees brightened nearly every wardroom and mess-deck of the High Seas Fleet that morning. This *Gemütlichkeit* tradition was so beloved in the Imperial Navy that a freighter had been pressed into service the previous day to take the boughs of greenery to ships at outer anchorages. 'We decorated them as best we could,' a seaman on the battleship *Helgoland* recorded in his diary, 'and that evening we stood around the lights, bright-eyed like children.'[1] Packages of oranges and nuts had been distributed to enlisted men.

But there was a grim streak beneath the fellowship and goodwill, for the fleet was expecting a British attack that day. In fact, it had been expecting such an attack for years. From their reading of British history, the men at the helm of the German navy were firmly convinced that a war with Britain would see an immediate Royal Navy descent in the Nelsonian tradition on the North Sea coast, to force a fleet action or establish a close blockade, or both.[2] This belief had been a major factor in the shaping of the Imperial Navy since the late 1890s, governing considerations of strategy and tactics, influencing warship design, even, as noted earlier, affecting the ratios of ship types. So strongly was this belief held that a later High Seas Fleet commander summed up Germany's entire naval strategy at the outbreak of war in a chapter title of a book as 'Awaiting the enemy's offensive'.[3]

But unknown to, or unaccepted by, the German naval hierarchy, the strategy of close investment had been abandoned by the Royal Navy in 1912 in favour of the policy of distant blockade of the entire North Sea – a policy that would ultimately result in Germany's economic strangulation. So, as day after day passed in early August without the expected attack, the Germans were baffled. The failure of the British battlefleet to appear during the 28 August engagement in the bight increased their confusion.

At the same time, this action inflicted a severe psychological defeat, for it reinforced an incipient sense of German maritime inferiority.

The absence of a British attack, the attitude engendered by the 28 August action, and Wilhelm II's strictures against risking the loss of capital ships combined to turn the Imperial Navy to the policy of maritime guerrilla warfare mentioned earlier, which involved submarine and mine ambushes, tip-and-run raids by the battlecruisers and occasional sorties by the fleet's main body in efforts to trap an inferior enemy force.

Even before this policy placed a premium on reconnaissance, protective scouting to detect the expected imminent arrival of the British fleet had been a vital need. At the outset of the war this had been provided by three patrol lines at fixed distances from the Elbe No 1 lightvessel. The innermost, 23 nautical miles out, was held by vessels of the minesweeping divisions, largely navy-requisitioned trawlers. Six miles farther out was a line patrolled by submarines; the outermost line at another six-mile interval was maintained by destroyers, stiffened by two to four light cruisers stationed east and south of Heligoland. In addition, naval-manned trawlers patrolled the estuaries, and battlecruisers or battleships were stationed as guard vessels at the river mouths. The destroyer and submarine patrols were maintained only during daylight hours.

This system had several defects. It did not extend far enough out to detect an enemy advance in time for the heavy units in the Jade or Elbe to reach the open sea; the constant patrolling inflicted material wear-and-tear on the destroyers and physical strain on their crews; it exposed the destroyers and cruisers to attack by superior forces before they could obtain big-gun support, as the 28 August action demonstrated, and also to attack by the British submarines that were active in the bight from the earliest days of the war.

Consequently, the sysem was changed after 28 August. Greater reliance was placed on trawlers and other small craft for routine patrol; larger numbers of these fishing vessels were navy-manned and they were pushed out farther into the bight. Heavy units continued to be used as river-mouth guard ships, but the destroyers, instead of maintaining day-long patrols, made sweeps at fixed intevals. Large minefields were laid west of Heligoland, the first of many planted by both sides that would eventually cover vast areas of the bight.

Such were the surface defences the Harwich Force would have to traverse for the Cuxhaven Raid. But more significant to the history of that raid were the German aerial defences. For the reasons outlined above, the High Seas Fleet began to rely heavily on aerial scouting. 'In our situation,' the 1916-18 commander of that fleet wrote, referring to the 1914 months, 'aeroplanes and airships played a particularly important part.'[4] But he continued, 'Unfortunately, their number was very small at the start.'[5]

How small those numbers were in terms of airships, even at the end of 1914 after the ambitious construction programme had been started, has been noted in Chapter 1. Their operational value was limited still more by the unavailability of bases. Of these, only Nordholz was complete and fully satisfactory. It is time for a look at this target toward which, as we left them, the British fliers were, they hoped, winging their way.

The Nordholz base, known to the British only by the approximate dimensions of its airship shed and even more vaguely by location, had become the headquarters of the Naval Airship Division in October. It would remain the division's HQ, except for a six-month period in 1917, until the end of the war. By then it boasted six airship hangars, but in 1914 there was only one, a structure that had been authorized in January, 1913. Code-named 'Nobel', it was a double shed comprising two hangars in one, each 597 feet long, 114 feet wide and 98 feet high.[6] The first hangar had been completed in August, 1914, and the second in November. The entire 4000-ton structure was mounted on a giant turntable that could swing it into any prevailing wind, a crucial consideration in the operation of airships, for a wind blowing at a contrary angle across a hangar's mouth could keep a ship immobilized inside for hours or even days at a time.

Other structures at the site included a hydrogen-generation plant, a gas storage reservoir ('gasometer') with a capacity of a million cubic feet, and barracks for a ground force that by the end of 1914 totalled somewhat more than 500 men. Such large numbers were needed for ground handling of airships, for in 1914 all such work was done manually. According to the leading historian of the German naval airship, protection of the base consisted of only a few machine guns and small arms,[7] but the German official naval history indicates there was at least one 'SK [Schnellfeuerkanone] Batterie' (battery of quick-firing cannon) somewhere in the vicinity.[8]

Only one other North Sea airship base was operational in 1914, a double shed at Fuhlsbüttel near Hamburg. This had been built in 1910 to house the craft flown by the German Airship Transportation Company in its previously described peacetime excursions, and had been rented for naval use since April, 1913.

With only four hangars available, only four of the six rigid airships possessed by the navy in December could be based for North Sea operations. They were the prewar $L3$ and its sisters commissioned since September, $L4$, $L5$ and $L6$. The four were identical: 518 feet long, lifted by a maximum 794,000 cubic feet of hydrogen, propelled by three motors with a combined 530 horsepower at speeds of 47-52 miles per hour. As of 23 December, $L3$ and $L4$ were based at Fuhlsbüttel, $L5$ and $L6$ at Nordholz.

Since the start of the war, the airships had made several scouting flights ranging as far as 300 miles over the sea, but had accomplished little of real value to the fleet. $L3$, as the Naval Airship Division's sole operational craft in August, had put in an appearance during the battle of 28 August, only to draw fire from German destroyers which the airshipmen misidentified as British cruisers, and then returning to base for 'technical reasons'[9] before being able to sight the British battlecruisers. $L6$ had gone aloft during the British advance into the bight on 24 November but had sighted nothing.

Worsening weather with the approach of winter severely limited airship operations, so much so that the Zeppelins had been totally idle during the first weeks of December. The first flights that month had not been possible until the 23rd. $L6$ and $L5$ had gone out from Nordholz on the 24th, but thick offshore clouds soon forced them to turn back. Otherwise, it is possible they might have sighted the Harwich Force during its advance. In a telephone conversation with $L6$'s captain that evening, the commander of the Naval Airship Division, Fregattenkapitän Strasser, authorized a patrol by that ship the next morning if weather permitted.

German naval aeroplane strength was also feeble at the start of the war. There was only one North Sea naval air station, at Heligoland, with a force of no more than six planes. Starting in early August, steps were taken to improve this situation. The Heligoland station was expanded, and by December other seaplane bases had been established at Borkum and at List on Sylt, largest of the German North Frisian Islands off the Schleswig coast.* Later expanded into a major base, List was no more than a fuelling station in 1914, but at least one seaplane was sheltering

---

* The northern Schleswig mainland was then German territory, having been conquered by Prussia during its 1864 war with Denmark. Later in the war a major airship base was established there, at Tondern (now Danish Toder). Northern Schleswig returned to Denmark after the war, as the result of a plebiscite under the Treaty of Versailles.

there on 25 December. A base had also been established on Norderney, but it was flooded out in September and was not operational for the rest of 1914. Wilhelmshaven was the naval air arm's headquarters and material depot.

By mid-December, the North Sea naval air force numbered perhaps as many as 20 aircraft, all floatplanes,* although not all of them were ever serviceable at one time. The motley assortment of seaplanes, largely foreign types, with which Germany had begun the war, had been replaced by domestic craft from a number of manufacturers. Most numerous in the North Sea were Friedrich-shafen FF 19 floatplanes produced by Flugzeugbau Friedrich-shafen GmbH. This firm was a subsidiary of the Zeppelin company, co-founded by Count von Zeppelin and one of his associates, Dr Theodore Kober, who was the aeroplane company's chief designer. Roughly comparable in performance to all but the latest model British Shorts, the FF 19 was similar in configuration – a single-engine, two-seater, twin-float biplane. It was powered by the 100-horsepower Mercedes, an engine that was remarkably reliable in an era when no aero engine was truly trustworthy. Towards the end of 1914 the FF 19 was being supplemented by the later, higher-powered (120hp Mercedes) FF 29 and FF 29a. There were also a few Albatros floatplanes, converted or modified versions of the type widely used for reconnaissance by the German army.

The seaplanes had played an inconspicuous role during the early months of the war. They were used to supplement the surface craft in reconnaissance and patrol in the bight, but were handicapped by their operational radius of no more than 75 nautical miles at best, and even more so by their lack of radios. The limitations of their value were demonstrated during the 28 August engagement when two planes went up from Heligoland. Their take-off was delayed by fog, and their crews although sighting some British ships, 'obtained no complete picture of the situation.'[11] Unable to communicate from the air, they had to return to Heligoland to impart their information and there they again ran into fog that delayed their landing. Their meagre reports were finally delivered far too late to have any bearing on the battle.

As British submarines became bothersome in the bight, the

---

* The German navy, unlike those of other major powers, did not look with favour on the flying boat and operated only a small number of such craft during 1914-18. Nor, unlike some other navies, did it use landplanes for over-water work. It did, however, paralleling the Royal Naval Air Service, operate some land squadrons on the Western Front.

German light cruiser *Stralsund*, unsuccessfully bombed by Charles H K Edmonds during the Cuxhaven Raid. She was one of only two German warships to be attacked that day. *US Naval Photographic Center*

German battlecruiser SMS *Von der Tann*, seen here probably during sea trials in 1910. She was one of the vessels that fired at British aircraft during the Cuxhaven Raid. *US Naval Photographic Center*

seaplanes were used to carry bombs on anti-submarine patrols. Several attacks were reported but none was successful and in one case the tables were turned when in September the British *E 3* surprised a seaplane on the water, apparently down with engine trouble, and captured its crew.[11]

Despite the continued failure of the Royal Navy to carry the war to Germany's coastline, German forebodings of such as attack mounted toward the end of 1914. Apprehension was spurred by various developments that became known to German naval intelligence. One was the vast naval construction programme inaugurated by Lord Fisher soon after his return to the Admiralty. Among the ships belonging to what Churchill called 'this tremendous new Navy, for it was nothing less,'[12] were monitors for close inshore bombardment and armoured infantry-landing craft, vessels that seemed to coincide ominously with Fisher's known advocacy of troop landings on German soil.

Since this programme had barely begun in November, its ramifications were a matter for concern in the future. A more immediate source of worry was seen in the regroupings of the Grand Fleet that followed Hipper's raid of 16 December. The German official naval history indicates that the shift of British battlecruisers south to Rosyth was interpreted not as the defensive measure it actually was, but as an offensive move designed to place Beatty's force within closer striking distance of Germany.

Another British defensive move was similarly misinterpreted. A number of old merchant vessels had been collected to sink as blockships to bar entrances of the Scapa Flow base to U-boats. Unaware of this intended purpose, the Germans thought these ships were to be employed in an effort to block the estuaries used by the High Seas Fleet. Although some audacious plans (which never got beyond the discussion stage) for operations against the German coast were considered at the Admiralty, nothing of this kind was ever seriously entertained. But for some months in late 1914 and early 1915 it seemed to German thinking that 'the idea was extremely probable' and 'success in it was by no means out of the question.'[13]

Adding these factors together, the German naval command came to the conclusion in late December that 'in the near future a major attack [grösser Angriff] against the ports or islands of the German [Heligoland] Bight was to be expected,'[14] and that it would probably be a blocking effort.

This assumption seemed to be confirmed on 24 December with

receipt of 'dependable information ... that the alleged blockading attack was imminent,'[15] and very likely to take place that day or the next. The German history does not reveal the source of the 'dependable information,' but there is little doubt that it came from spies.[16]

Immediate steps were taken to alert the fleet to the expected attack. Ships were 'issued a special warning about enemy merchant vessels which were camouflaged as warships and would probably cooperate with submarines.'[17] This would seem to indicate that German agents had been able to note the empty berths of the Harwich submarine flotilla, and since there was no reason for blockships to masquerade as warships, may also indicate that spies were aware of the seaplane carriers but did not know what they actually were. (We will note later some further indications of German ignorance about the carriers.)

In addition to alerting the Heligoland Bight patrols to increased vigilance, the naval authorities supplemented protective scouting by ordering two submarines out. One was to be stationed off Borkum to watch the entrances to the Ems, the other to patrol between the North Frisian island of Amrum, just south of Sylt, and Heligoland to the south-west. Both were to keep look-out that afternoon and between 3am and twilight of the 25th. Destroyers were ordered to raise steam for sailing at one-and-a-half-hours notice, and other warships placed on three-hour notice. The usual system of guard ships and patrols was to be adhered to.

While these defensive orders were issued promptly, there is a strange element of passivity to them. No active measures were taken except for reinforcing the patrol lines with submarines – and two U-boats were a totally inadequate number to cover the areas through which the British might pass. Stranger still, it seems that no special warning was given to the airship or seaplane branches of the naval air arm on the 24th. At Fuhlsbüttel, Zeppelin L 3 was taken out of service that day for modification of its control surfaces, hardly something that would have been done if the Naval Airship Division had been expecting action the next day.

The daylight and evening hours of 24 December passed with no sign of a British attack. There was only one incident: U 6, the submarine assigned to cover the Amrum-Heligoland gap, reported she had twice sighted an enemy submarine, but it had submerged both times before it could be attacked. At nightfall the U 6's commander, Oberleutnant zur See Lepsius, took his boat down to rest on the sea bottom in the vicinity of the last sighting, hoping to catch the British vessel by surprise when and if it surfaced in the morning. The value of a U-boat as a counter-weapon to enemy underwater craft had already been demonstrated when on 18 November the *E 3*, captor of the seaplane in September, had been destroyed by *U 27*.

The *U 6* report was no cause for special alarm. British submarines had infested the bight for months, and there was no reason to presume that Lepsius had encountered anything out of the ordinary.

The early hours of Christmas Day found the vessels of the High Seas Fleet disposed at customary ports and anchorages, with several guard ships out and alerted for the supposedly impending attack. Standing off the Jade were battlecruisers *Von der Tan* and *Moltke*, to be relieved at daylight by battlecruisers *Derfflinger* and *Seydlitz*. Stationed in the Elbe were three old pre-dreadnoughts of Battle Squadron IV, *Wittelsbach*, *Wettin* and *Mecklenburg*. Seaward of the first two of these, stretched across the estuary as an anti-submarine screen, were the five destroyers of Half-Flotilla III.* The destroyers of Half-Flotilla XII were returning to the Jade from a pre-dawn patrol that had sighted nothing. In the Jade, other destroyers of Flotilla VII were preparing for a daylight patrol. Flotilla I was scheduled to sail at daybreak to investigate mines reported off Heligoland some days earlier. A minesweeping division also was to go out.

But while the fleet was thus on the alert, an aerial attack was probably the last thing in the world it expected that morning. Although there had been an air raid scare on the very first day of the war, with wild reports of a bomb dropped on the Wilhelm-shaven town hall,[18] this sort of hysteria had quickly abated. Even the simplest seaman soon came to believe that the High Seas Fleet's bases were far beyond the reach of enemy aircraft, while at the same time taking satisfaction and pride in the fleet's own air strength as symbolized by the mighty airships.[19] The existence of ships able to take nascent Royal Navy air power to sea apparently was unrealized. The carriers had not been sighted during their two previous unsuccessful raiding attempts, and when they were finally seen on 25 December they appeared at first so novel as to defy identification.

Despite Tyrwhitt's fears, the Harwich Force had been unde-

---

* A destroyer half-flotilla (Halbflottille) was the equivalent of the British destroyer division and was customarily composed of four or five ships. Two half-flotillas formed a flotilla. The Royal Navy destroyer flotilla of World War I was much larger, with a usual strength of 16 or 20 vessels in four or five 4-ship divisions.

tected during its approach. Whatever the ships encountered around 4am, no warning had been given about the British squadron. They were probably merely peaceful fishing vessels, numbers of which were continuing their indispensable work in the bight. Nor is there any explanation for the numerous radio messages overheard on *Arethusa*, except a guess they were routine traffic.

Strangely, around 5am the Germans also picked up strong radio traffic which was assumed to be enemy.[20] Its source is equally mysterious, for the British ships were observing strict radio silence.

The British were not the only ones seeing mysterious lights that morning, either. Around 5am, *U 6*, popping up to carry out the hoped-for ambush of the enemy submarine seen the day before, 'observed a strong white light near the Amrum Bank'[21] close to the location where the supposed British vessel had last submerged. At 5.12am a message was received from *Lepsius*, relayed from Heliogoland, that *U 6*, on the basis of this sighting, had encountered a 'suspicious vessel.'[22] It was assumed the light was being shown by a submarine or other ship as a beacon to guide an enemy force approaching from the north – an ingenious guess, but the British were not employing any such procedure.

Oddly, at about the same time the battleship *Mecklenburg* also observed a similar light. The German official history, although backing the beacon theory, concedes that what both submarine and battleship may have seen was a light being shown by one of the patrol trawlers, and this appears the most logical explanation.

At any rate, it now seemed that something was going on out in the bight. Tension mounted when at 5.30am the battleship *Wettin* mistook in the mists of the Elbe a patrol trawler for an enemy submarine and opened fire on it. Only a few shots were fired before the error was realized, and the trawler did not suffer 'any important damage'[23], a statement implying that *some* damage was inflicted. These were the only shots fired by one surface vessel at another during the entire day's action.

The noise of *Wettin's* gunfire booming over the Elbe alarmed and alerted other ships and shore stations. Her shots were an accidental but effective curtain-raiser for the ensuing drama. About an hour later, as the sun began to rise, the haze that caused *Wettin's* mistaken identification intensified, soon forming a thick curtain over the coastal plains. The coastline itself was mostly clear during the forenoon, as were the estuary mouths, but inland the fog massed into a grey blanket extending in some areas down to ground level, veiling in obscurity towns, villages and ships at inner ports and anchorages. During the morning it would shift and thin from time to time over some areas, leaving them alternately clear and then cloaked in invisibility.

To the eastward, the fog was even thicker and lower. Weather conditions at the airship base at Fuhlsbüttel were bad, making it impossible for L 4, hangar partner of the immobilized L 3, to leave the ground. Nordholz, however, where fog alternated with fair skies that morning, was clear around sunrise, and at 6.31am L 6 lifted off for the previously authorized morning patrol.

Out at sea, the weather remained clear and bright with excellent visibility. As the sun rose, Lepsius in U 6 saw clouds of smoke to the north, and at 7.30am could see masts and funnels appearing over the horizon. Closing, he could discern the approaching vessels were British and even, the German official history indicates, identify them by class, 'Two ... cruisers of the Arethusa type, eight destoyers of the 'L' class, three ships painted grey, the derricks swung out, large superstructures at the stern, no doubt, they were aircraft carriers!'[24]

U 6 submerged for an attempt to attack 'the second cruiser',[25] presumably Undaunted, which had put on speed to close with the squadron from her rearguard position and was the rear-most ship. But just as Lepsius was lining her up in his periscope, the British force veered six to eight points west and steamed rapidly away from the submarine. The U-boat skipper surfaced, rigged radio aerials to report what he had seen, and then set out in pursuit. Near the Eider lightvessel Lepsius was distracted by a more inviting target – what appeared to be the conning tower of a submarine suddenly surfacing on the starboard beam. It disappeared again below water before U 6 could manoeuvre into attacking position. The boat's look-outs then became confused by smoke from nearby fishing vessels. After milling about a while, U 6 gave up the chase of an enemy that was now impossible to catch at a submarine's slow surface speed, returned to her patrol station to the north, and vanishes from the history of the Cuxhaven Raid.

While it has often been stated that U 6's contact report was the first warning of the British presence, the German official history says the initial alarm came somewhat earlier (how much earlier is not reported) from Heligoland, where look-outs sighted the enemy squadron at 20 nautical miles off the island.[26] At any rate, by 7.30am or shortly afterward, a general alert ordering 'intensive readiness' had been issued by the German naval command. At 7.49am L 5 lifted off from Nordholz, and within a few minutes seaplanes began to take to the air from Heligoland, Borkum and List.

Despite *U 6*'s supposed but highly dubious identification of some of the British ships as carriers,[27] the Germans were still unaware that what they were about to face was not an advance by block-ships but an aerial attack. The first to realize this were the crew of the 273-ton trawler *Wega*, a unit of the Jade-Weser Harbour Defence Flotilla. At 7.35am they saw five seaplanes heading south, apparently on course for the Elbe. Unfortunately, the only radio-equipped boat in *Wega*'s patrol group was absent that morning, laid up for repairs, so there was no way to deliver an immediate report. The best that could be done was to dispatch another trawler, the 185-ton *Seefahrt*, to the nearest lightvessel, which could radio the report to Heligoland. For unexplained reasons there was a delay of nearly an hour in this vital transmission. By then *Wega*'s report had been overtaken by events, but when it did arrive it was 'the first really complete one reaching the naval command'[28] about the impending aerial attack.

Before this, however, the British aircraft had begun to appear over the coastline and rivers. Ten minutes after the *Wega*'s sighting, a seaplane suddenly arrived above the Elbe, flying over destroyer *S 131* of Half-Flotilla III at scarcely more than 250 feet. The destroyer and battleship *Wittelsbach* fired off a few shots at it without effect, the day's first gunfire at an aerial target.

At 8am a second plane was spotted over Scharhörn Reef, the extremity of a large sand bank jutting out along the western entrance to the Elbe and lying about 15 miles north-west of Cuxhaven. This craft veered off after a few shots from various ships. Twelve minutes later, *L 5*, over the Weser, saw three seaplanes, and at 8.30 yet another was sighted and fired upon over the Grosser Vogel Sand at the mouth of the Elbe. About the same time two planes were observed from the forts at Geeste-münde on the Weser near Bremerhaven, seemingly headed on a course for Nordholz.

At 8.40, as the confusing reports continued to pour in, the destroyers of Half-Flotilla IV reinforced those of Half-Flotilla III in the Elbe. By now the air raid alarm had been flashed all along the northern coast, and defence posts were standing on alert as far away as Kiel.

For a number of German sailors, airmen and coastal gunners, Christmas morning was about to prove less than festive.

Douglas A Oliver who flew Short Type 74 No 815 from *Empress* in the Cuxhaven Raid. *Fleet Air Arm Museum*

CHAPTER 7

Thick Banks of Fog ...
All Over the Land

It took the British seaplanes the better part of an hour to reach the German coast. A few of them kept in sight of others during the first stage of the flight, but their varying speeds and different take-off times soon combined to separate them into seven individual adventures.

The experiences of their ten occupants were uniform for the first half hour or so. All pilots sighted Heligoland after take-off and soon encountered trawlers below, some sailing in formation. During this period two pilots saw a phenomenon that remains another of the Cuxhaven Raid's mysteries – what appeared to be a British seaplane disabled on the water. A misinterpretation was prompted by this that will be discussed later.

As the seaplanes drew nearer the coast, destroyers and other warships could be seen. Some of these challenged by flashing searchlights followed by ineffective gunfire when the signals went unanswered.

Between 7.10am and 8.12am all the pilots reported seeing a German airship, and some caught sight of two. These were glimpses of *L 6*, heading for Heligoland through high scattered clouds that now were forming over the bight, or *L 5*, flying farther to the west. Some pilots fleetingly considered attacking the enemy craft, but that could have been done only by dropping bombs from above and even when the seaplanes were not already at an altitude disadvantage, the British fliers realized they could never outclimb an airship. Two pilots called one of the airships a Schütte-Lanz. This misidentification, which would be repeated later that day, is puzzling, for a Schütte-Lanz and a Zeppelin were virtually indistinguishable except at quite close range, but it showed that the British were now far more knowledgeable about German airship types than they had been a few months before.*

* Shape and placement of control and engine cars, and configuration of tail fins, were the main external differences between the two types. The first naval Schütte-Lanz was not commissioned until February 1915.

The airship sightings were the first indication the good luck that had attended the British so far was deserting them now. Even before most of the pilots had crossed the coastline, their intended prey was aloft and immune to them. There remained as a target the airship base itself, where the British mistakenly believed two more Zeppelins might be sheltering, and where the hydrogen supply might be devastatingly touched-off.

On a clear day there would have been no difficulty in spotting this target. The reflection of the morning sun on the towering walls of the huge hangar could be seen for a dozen miles, a blazing beacon that would have been visible to the British pilots as soon as they reached the vicinity of Cuxhaven.[1] But there was no such gleaming guide this morning; instead, as the seaplanes approached shore, ahead of them loomed the grey murk that would frustrate all the British hopes. The pilots' report describe it with dreary repetition, 'Thick banks of fog ahead and all over the land', 'a thick ground fog drifting in masses', 'the land ... completely covered with a low-lying mist, which blotted out everything except what was lying immediately under the machine.'[2] Some pilots, coming in over the relatively clear estuary mouths, encountered the fog a few minutes later than others, but as they flew inland all were soon engulfed. They were forced to fly increasingly low in the hope of picking up some visual clue to the airship base's whereabouts, or simply to see anything at all on the ground.

Because of the confusion created by the fog, and because many of the times given by the pilots, who had to jot them down hurriedly in their cockpits or recall them later, are merely estimates, it is next to impossible to ascertain where the planes were at specific times that morning. It is equally difficult to correlate the British reports with German accounts, for the Germans also were confused by the fog. In some instances a single plane seen briefly from the ground at three spots might be reported as three separate planes.

With these caveats in mind, let us try to trace as best we can the wanderings of the seven seaplanes in their search for the 'Cuxhaven' base through an all-too-literal fog of war.

It is a fairly safe bet that Short No 135 from *Riviera*, flown by Flight Commander Francis E T Hewlett,* was the first plane

---

* Hewlett was the only son of novelist/essayist/poet Maurice Hewlett (1861-1923), whose historical romances such as *The Forest Lovers* and *The Queen's Quair* were extremely popular in the first years of this century and are almost totally forgotten today. His mother, Hilda, was the first woman to receive the Royal

sighted by the Germans, the one fired upon by *S 131* and *Wittelsbach*. Hewlett encountered fog earlier than most of the other pilots, as far out as Sharnhörn Reef and the island of Neuwark, neither of which he could see. Even to glimpse water he had to descend to 200 feet, where the sea was just visible. Continuing at this altitude, at 7.44am he 'sighted a battleship or armoured cruiser'[3] which opened fire. The altitude and time coincide closely to those given in the German account of the aircraft sightings by *S 131* and *Wittelsbach*. Hewlett apparently did not see the destroyer.

'I soon got out of sight,' Hewlett reported, 'shortly afterwards nearly fouling the masts of three or four large cruisers, who opened fire immediately.'[4] Hastily consulting one of the charts Childers had prepared, the pilot judged that the only water deep enough for ships that size was just off Cuxhaven, so he altered course south to fly inland. After five minutes the fog cleared enough for Hewlett to see he was over land, but there were no recognizable landmarks. By 8.05am he considered he must have been near the airship base, but could find nothing and flying under 200 feet lost sight of the ground completely. He wrote, 'I realized that it would be useless to drop my bombs,'[5] and so three minutes later he changed course to return to sea.

At 8.20 the fog cleared and Hewlett found himself over water with nothing in sight in any direction. Ten minutes later he spotted what seemed to be a destroyer and dropped to 500 feet to examine it, but it was making too much smoke to identify. Now judging he had overshot the Frisian Islands, he turned south again and at 8.40 saw an airship emerge from a cloud to the south and 1500 feet above him. This was undoubtedly *L 5*, whose movements will be described later, and Hewlett mistakenly thought it fired at him 'with rifle or small gun.'[6] Actually, his plane apparently was not even seen from the Zeppelin.

At 9.12am, still not having seen islands or land, Hewlett reversed course to the north once more, hoping he was on 'the correct bearing for meeting the seaplane carriers and the flotilla.'[7]

Flight Commander Robert P Ross, piloting Folder No 119 from *Engadine*, found the mouth of the Elbe clear enough at 7.40am to

Aero Club aviator's certificate. Hewlett, who became a naval cadet in 1904, learned to fly in 1911 at a flight school operated by Mrs Hewlett and Gustave Blondeau, and later transferred to the RNAS – the only naval aviator who 'had been taught to fly by his mother.' 'His technical knowledge, due to long experience of aviation,' *Riviera's* Robertson wrote later, 'was exceeded by very few' in 1914.

make out from 2000 feet eight anchored merchant ships and what he thought might be a hospital ship, then two destroyers, 'one of which fired at me, but the shot passed below.'[8]

After this the fog closed in and he could see nothing for the next ten minutes as he flew south-west, gradually descending to 500ʳ feet. At 7.50am, 'thinking I should be about abreast of the sheds,'[9] he turned east but had to go down to 150 feet before the ground was visible. There was nothing to be seen as he 'cruised about over sand dunes and sand.'[10] At this point he discovered

> The pressure system in the seaplane was leaking badly, and I could get no petrol into my gravity tank, and realizing that I should probably run out of petrol in a quarter of an hour, deemed it advisable to make for the water again, in case I had to land.[11]

At 8.30am in the vicinity of Wangeroog Island, Ross sighted what seemed to be a submarine diving. He dropped a bomb ahead of the vessel's presumed underwater track, but it failed to explode. His target remains a mystery; it is unlikely that it was a submarine.

The mechanical trouble now became so alarming that Ross landed to examine the pressure system. While he was doing so, 'I observed a trawler coming for me at full speed, started my engine and ran away from her and escaped into the haze.'[12] That danger past, he managed to get the pressure pump working well enough to keep fuel in the gravity tank, took off and shaped course for the carrier rendezvous.

Flight Lieutenant Arnold J Miley, in *Engadine*'s Folder No 120, reached the coastline at 8.10am and found that the fog, although thick, did not totally restrict his view. He crossed and recrossed a railway line, observing nothing more than two villages, many ploughed fields and a number of farms. 'In spite of covering a good deal of ground I found no [airship] sheds and no fortified places worth attacking.'[13] At 8.30 he turned north and recrossed the coastline, coming under fire from a shore battery he could not see.

Miley apparently tried to carry out the requested reconnaissance of Wilhelmshaven but missed it in the fog, emerging in the vicinity of the Jade entrance. For the next 20 minutes or so, until he reached Wangeroog, he was fired at by a variety of ships in the Jade and the Weser and Schillig Roads. He identified them as three light cruisers at the Weser's mouth, two more steaming up the river, and another two entering the Jade; a battlecruiser at Schillig Roads, and a destroyer flotilla entering the Jade. 'All ships challenged me with a searchlight,' he reported, 'and all fired with anti-aircraft guns, apparently, as I was too high for the elevation of any ordinary naval guns and all shells ... were time-fused.'[14]

At 9.05am Miley was five miles north of Wangeroog, where he turned west and passed over two trawlers. Ten minutes later he sighted an airship, probably *L 5*, which he misidentified as a Schütte-Lanz, heading west at 4000 feet. At 9.30 he was six miles east of Norderney.

Flight Commander Douglas A Oliver, flying Short Type 74 No 815 from *Empress*, with Chief Petty Officer Budds as observer, ran into fog about 7.40am after sighting the Elbe lightships and had to drop from 2000 feet down to 700. He emerged into a clear area directly above the five destroyers of Half-Flotilla III. They flashed a searchlight challenge and then opened fire which Oliver avoided by turning west and climbing again to 2000 feet into the fog. A few minutes later he went back to 700 feet and found himself over Neuwark, coming under fire from guns that seemed to be on the island. The Short's tailplane was hit.

Oliver turned south again and ten minutes later, thinking he must be nearly opposite the airship base to the east, headed in that direction to hunt for it. After being fired at from the ground again, the pilot 'sighted railway; searched up and down; sighted Cuxhaven, but could find no trace of sheds.'[15]

After 35 minutes of fruitless search, Oliver gave up and headed west to reconnoitre Schillig Roads. Flying over the Weser, he and Budds saw two light cruisers and a number of destroyers, 'All opened fire, but without effect.'[16] At 9.35am two battlecruisers in the Jade joined in firing at the plane. Ten minutes later the Short reached Wangeroog and Oliver turned west. On Langeoog Island he observed a row of sheds he thought might be a seaplane base. All three bombs were dropped on these, and the second apparently destroyed one of them. Since there was no seaplane base on the island, Oliver's target probably was a group of fishermen's sheds or warehouses.

With bombs gone and fuel running low, Oliver continued west, reaching Norderney shortly after 10am and turning north to seek the carriers.*

Riviera's Type 74 No 811, flown by Flight Lieutenant Charles H

* The British aviation journalist C G Grey, writing in *The Aeroplane* of 12 October 1939 (an article reprinted in *United States Naval Institute Proceedings* 65, No 442, December 1939, pp 1806-10), stated that Oliver, in a fit of frustration after his bombs were expended, hurled his golliwog mascot at the battlecruiser *Von der Tann*. Oliver's report shows this amusing story could not possibly be true.

K Edmonds, reached land without receiving the gunfire reception accorded most of the other British planes, but was soon equally engulfed in the fog. Edmonds had to stay at 250 feet to see the ground. He found the Bremerhaven–Cuxhaven railway, the same guide used by other pilots, and followed it southward for seven miles. 'Not sighting the sheds,' he reported' 'I steered to the eastward for about 5 miles and then to the northward for about 10 miles.'[17]

At this point he decided to give up the search, for 'time was getting short,'[18] the fog showed no sign of clearing, and even if he had found a target the low altitude at which he was forced to fly would not have given the fusing mechanisms in his bombs time to arm them before they struck.

Turning west, Edmonds emerged into clear skies over the coast and sighted in the Weser two light cruisers, one with four funnels, the other with three, which he decided to attack. He climbed to 1000 feet and headed for the ships in a shallow dive, pulling out and releasing bombs at 800 feet as the cruisers opened fire with cannon, machine guns and rifles.

His targets were the light cruisers *Stralsund* (the four-funnelled vessel) and *Graudenz*. According to the German account of the attack, it occurred at 8.30am and the Short bombed from a slightly higher altitude (between 984 and 1312 feet) than stated by Edmonds.[19] Edmonds' report indicates he released all three bombs, but the German history accounts for only two, one going wild, the other exploding about 200 yards off *Graudenz*' beam and sending up a 30-foot column of water. The pilot himself was unable to observe their fall.

The cruisers' anti-aircraft fire was heavy and accurate: the Germans saw the right wing of the Short 'pierced through repeatedly,'[20] and Edmonds later counted six hits, five by bullets, one by shrapnel. As Edmonds sped on to the south the machine gun and rifle fire ceased but the heavier-calibre guns kept up a fusillade. He came under more rifle fire a few minutes later from an estimated twelve merchant vessels, flying the German naval ensign, near the Hoheweg lighthouse.

Now, as Edmonds' fuel gauge dipped lower and lower, he calculated there was no time left to reconnoitre Wilhelmshaven, so he headed for Wangeroog to start the return leg of the flight. On the way to the island he got a good view of the ships at Schillig Roads, and later reported the heavy units lying there as two battlecruisers, another two-funnelled vessel, either a battle-cruiser or an armoured cruiser, and a four-funnelled armoured cruiser which he correctly guessed was the *Roon*. There were also two smaller cruisers entering the Jade, and numerous tugs and other small craft at the river entrance.

After coming under shellfire near Wangeroog and spotting an airship near the entrance to the Weser, Edmonds continued without incident to Norderney and turned north. Although he did not yet know it, he had been the only British pilot to attack enemy ships that day.*

The flight of Type 74 No 814 from *Empress*, piloted by Flight Sub-Lieutenant Vivian Gaskell Blackburn with his mechanic, Chief Petty Officer James Bell, as observer, is the most puzzling to follow. The report by Gaskell Blackburn, who was the lowest-ranking of the seven pilots, gives no times for any incidents of the flight and only the vaguest of locations.

After coming under fire from trawlers and destroyers, Gaskell Blackburn ran into fog that 'rendered navigation extremely difficult',[21] so much so that he was unable to tell where he crossed the coastline. Sighting railway tracks (persumably the Bremerhaven–Cuxhaven line) he flew about six miles south of it and was the target of some ground fire, then searched to the north and south for the target, vainly burning up fuel in the fog. Finally, 'I determined to try and get back to the opposite side of the Jade River and return by the coast past Wangeroog,'[22] and headed south-west. This course must have taken him over the Weser, but apparently he did not sight it at all in the fog before reaching the Jade, where he 'came out of the mist over a four-funnelled cruiser ... and two three-funnelled cruisers under weigh.'[23]

To the north-west Gaskell Blackburn noted a number of destroyers steaming seaward and what appeared to be a British seaplane heading the same direction. Also to the north, Bell observed, were three battlecruisers and about fifteen other vessels, all making heavy smoke.

The first three cruisers 'opened an extremely hot anti-aircraft fire,'[24] as did the battlecruisers as the Short flew between the two groups of ships. The German fire was quite accurate for height, but the shells burst behind the planes. He reported, 'I came then to the outskirts of Wilhelmshaven and was again subjected to an extremely hot anti-aircraft fire ... the most accurate and fiercest

---

* In August, 1915, Edmonds carried out history's first aerial torpedo attack, again under Malone's command, flying from *Ben-my-Chree*. Formation of the Royal Air Force in April 1918, found him in command of the RNAS No 6 Wing, a seaplane unit, at Otranto, Italy. Transferring to the new service, he rose to the rank of air vice marshal.

fire during the trip.'[24] A small-calibre shell or a large metal fragment from a heavier missile tore through a main float and damaged a starboard undercarriage strut, damage Bell could see by peering from his cockpit.[26] Gaskell Blackburn aimed two bombs at what he believed was the land battery responsible; it 'did not fire again, and my observer reported that he thought we did damage it.'[27]

Continuing on over Wilhelmshaven, Gaskell Blackburn dropped his last bomb on what he reported as the middle of the city. Although he reported he heard all three bombs 'detonate satisfactorily from the low altitude which I was flying,'[28] there is no mention in the German official history of any bomb explosions in the vicinity of Wilhelmshaven.

With time and fuel running short, Gaskell Blackburn decided not to take the return route via Wangeroog and the other Frisian islands, but headed west-north-west over the mainland. The fog closed in again during this inland flight, forcing him to keep to 700 feet. Every time the Short emerged into a momentarily clear patch of sky, he reported, it was fired at by anti-aircraft guns or rifles: 'the country ... is infested with anti-aircraft guns.'[29]

Gaskell Blackburn reached the coast near Baltrum Island, Norderney's neighbour to the east, emerging into clear sky, quickly recognizing Norderney and heading north to seek the carriers.

The final flight to be recorded is that of Short No 136 from *Riviera*, the craft piloted by Flight Commander Cecil F Kilner with Childers as observer. As a bombing mission it was no more successful than any of the others, but it was the most rewarding observation flight of the day.

In their joint report, Kilner and Childers state they reached the coast at 8.17am at an altitude of 1000 feet. Immediately inland they were engulfed in the fog and had to reduce height to 200–300 feet to obtain visibility of no more than a half-mile: 'The fields were under hoar frost and the atmosphere was dull and dark.'[30] They were beset by another problem, 'Shortly after crossing the coastline, the engine began to misfire, possibly due to the extreme moisture of the atmosphere or to over lubrication.'[31] This trouble plagued them for the rest of the flight, with the engine sometimes dropping to 800 revolutions a minute from its rated 1300.

Kilner and Childers are the only airmen to say the airship base was believed to be 'a few miles to the eastward of the village of Cappel,'[32] which may be a mis-spelling of Cappsiel. Passing over what they believed to be this village, they searched to the east and south of it without success. Very soon, however, 'the state of the engine ... made it imperative to abandon the search for the sheds and regain water, as it was feared that it would be necessary to alight.'[33] They reached the coast over the Hoheweg Sand to the east of the Jade's main channel. Now the fog was left behind and the faltering engine suddenly perked up, permitting the Short to climb to 1500 feet as Kilner headed west-north-west toward Schillig Roads. But it began to sputter erratically again just before the plane reached the southern part of the anchorage.

As the Short flew up the middle of the fairway the vessels there opened an intense and accurate fire at it, 'The fusing was excellent, bursts occurring frequently just at our level.'[33] Shell fragments or shrapnel severed two rigging wires and damaged an undercarriage strut.

While Kilner nursed the seaplane through this barrage, Childers made a count of the ships in sight, accurately identifying battlecruisers *Seydlitz*, *Moltke* and *Von der Tann*, and armoured cruiser *Roon*. He noted seven battleships, but mistakenly reported them as units of the *Deutschland* and *Braunschweig* classes. Actually, these pre-dreadnoughts, which composed Battle Squadron II of the High Seas Fleet in 1914, were at Brunsbüttel on Christmas Day. Childers also made out vessels that he later reported as two old light cruisers, ten destroyers, a large freighter or liner and three possible colliers.

Although it has frequently been stated that Kilner and Childers attempted to bomb *Von der Tann* or some other ships in the Roads, their report says, 'No bombs were dropped on these vessels as a hit did not seem practicable, and it was considered advisable to reserve them for the submarine depot which was thought to be at Wangeroog.'[34]

As the Short left the fairway behind, Childers got a distant view of some merchant vessels and two cruisers in the Weser and two destroyers east of Wangeroog. Skirting that island, where no sign of the reported submarine base could be seen, Kilner turned west to follow the island chain seaward to Norderney. The eastern end of that island was reached at 9.36am and four minutes later Kilner shaped course north.

The weather that so frustrated the British fliers prevented the Germans from obtaining a coherent picture of the numbers or purpose of their phantom visitors in the fog. The air became alive with conflicting and confusing radio messages as reports of aircraft seen as different times and locations poured in from ships and shore stations. Emerging momentarily into clear patches and then vanishing again into the fog, the same plane might be seen twice or more and each time reported as a different craft. The heavy radio traffic added to the confusion, interfering with more reliable reports from ships able to see the aircraft clearly.[35]

The murk served to shield the planes from German gunfire. Some ships apparently fired blind into the fog in the direction of engine noise, but most waited until the aircraft emerged into such clear areas as the mouths of the Weser and Jade. Anti-aircraft fire, as noted by the British fliers, was heavy and uncomfortably accurate in those areas, especially the latter. There the planes were fired upon by all four of the battlecruisers that had been changing station, and by destroyers of Flotilla VII and of Half-Flotilla XII, the latter re-entering the Jade at 7.30am after a patrol of the bight. From a position off Hookfiel in Schillig Roads, the dreadnought *Ostfriesland*, which had been equipped with two 3.4-inch anti-aircraft guns at the beginning of the war, joined in.*

Fire was also poured into the sky from coastal batteries, including, as some British fliers thought, one on Wangeroog, which had been unfortified when the war began. In some instances, though, as at the Geestemünde forts, the planes appeared and vanished too quickly for them to be recognized as enemy.

All the British pilots shared Miley's belief that they were fired at by anti-aircraft guns instead of ordinary naval ordnance, and probably would have endorsed Gaskell Blackburn's opinion that the German coast was 'infested' with such guns. Actually, there were very few true anti-aircraft guns in the High Seas Fleet, or anywhere in Germany, in December 1914. The truth was that the low altitudes at which the British flew – in some cases, according to the German account, at no more than 300 feet over the Jade – brought them within the angle of elevation of small-calibre guns of the ships and forts, especially when the planes were low on the horizon.** The accuracy of the fire noted by the British pilots was simply a result of superior German fire control techniques and equipment, a superiority that would take such a heavy British toll at Jutland.

The most baffling incident of the raid remains to be told. It was what appeared to be the accomplishment of a mission sought by

* This was *Ostfriesland*'s first exposure to hostile aircraft. Her last occurred seven years later, when she was sunk by US Army planes off Cape Henry, Virginia, in experiments with aerial bombing of warships.

** The 3.4-inch guns that were the tertiary armament of the battleships and the main armament of most German destroyers in 1914 could be elevated to 25 degrees. The German anti-aircraft guns of the same calibre could be elevated to 60 degrees if fitted with a shield, or to 80 degrees without a shield.

the British – an attack on the Nordholz airship base.

Although the base had been clear at dawn, the fog began to close in soon after *L 5* took off, and the skies over it were alternately fair and clouded for the rest of the morning as the mist drifted. At 8.20am an aeroplane engine was heard in the murk, but nothing could be seen from the base. Ten minutes later, during a momentarily clear interval, a British seaplane emerged from the fog at an altitude of slightly under 1000 feet. A nearby battery (whether cannon or machine gun is unclear) opened up on it as it flew directly toward the giant hangar. As ground troops opened fire with machine guns and rifles, it changed direction and appeared to head for the 'gasometer'. A moment later it dropped two bombs that fell into the nearby wood, and then vanished in the fog, seemingly unharmed by the ground fire.[36]

The Germans were convinced at the time – and remained convinced when the official naval history recounting the incident was published nine years later – that this was a deliberate attempt to destroy the base's hydrogen supply. And from it the conclusion was correctly drawn later that the base was the objective of the British raid.

In fact, however, it was not a deliberate attack and there is no way to account for it. Not one of the British pilots laid eyes on the base or attacked it. Which plane was it, then, and why were the bombs dropped?

Portions of Gaskell Blackburn's report correlate with the German account. He was fired upon while well inland, and was the only pilot to report dropping bombs on inland targets. But according to his report, which gives no times for those incidents, the second of them took place near Wilhelmshaven. This location seems to be confirmed by his identification of the ships he and his observer saw shortly before he released his bombs. Unless Gaskell Blackburn's report is completely inaccurate, his plane must be ruled out as the one that appeared over Nordholz.

The only feasible explanation is that the bombs dropped there were released by one of the other pilots, who did not see the hangar, to lighten weight before heading back out to sea. But which pilot? Some can be eliminated. Hewlett reported deliber-ately *not* releasing his bombs inland. Oliver's three were dropped after his search for the base, as were Edmonds'. Kilner and Childers indicate their three were still in the racks as they started the return flight.

Ross, however, reported dropping only one after leaving the mainland, with no indication what became of the other two. And Miley, alone of the seven pilots, failed to report dropping a bomb at all.

Altogether, 10 bombs were released during the raid, leaving 11 unaccounted for. It is quite possible that some or all of the 11 remained in their racks during the return flights; it was not terribly dangerous to land with bombs in place, since they had to fall a certain distance before their impact fuses were armed. But it is more reasonable to assume that, with time growing short and fuel running low, they were jettisoned over either land or sea to rid the planes of useless weight. Malone's orders had given permission for this: 'In the event of a pilot considering that he cannot efficiently reach Cuxhaven, he must be guided by his own discretion as to whether any bombs are discarded, etc.'[37] However, not a single pilot reported jettisoning bombs for this reason, although perhaps this was considered too trivial to mention.

One can only guess that the bombs the Germans thought were aimed at the airship base were dropped at random by either Ross or Miley to lighten weight, and it was sheer chance that they fell near the base. But that *is* only a guess; the incident at Nordholz, the closest the British, unknowingly, came to achieving their objective, remains the greatest mystery of the Cuxhaven Raid.

Robert P Ross (left) and Arnold J Miley (right) in a photograph which appeared in the HMS *Engadine* Reunion Programme published in 1939. Both men were pilots of Folders in the Cuxhaven Raid. *Fleet Air Arm Museum*

CHAPTER 8

I Wish All Ships a Merry Christmas

As the events of Christmas morning unfolded, the response of the High Seas Fleet remained curiously passive. Not a single ship moved seaward; on the contrary, the advance patrol boats in the bight were ordered to withdraw to the outer roads of the estuaries, and the vessels scheduled to leave the port that day, destroyer Flotillas I and III and a minesweeping division, were held back.

The only positive action taken was to strengthen the river defences. The six ancient coast defence ships of Battle Squadron VI* were ordered to the Jade, and at 8.50am, shortly after the Elbe destroyer line had been reinforced, the pre-dreadnoughts of Battle Squadron II (the vessels that Childers mistakenly identified as being at Schillig Roads and which were actually lying in the Kiel Canal at Brunsbüttel) were ordered to the Altenbruch anchorage. By that time, however, the fog had thickened so much that navigation of the tortuous Elbe channel was too risky, so these battleships remained behind the canal lock-gates.

The vessels best placed and best prepared to engage the British squadron, the four battlecruisers of Scouting Squadron I, were leashed. The commanders of *Moltke* and *Von der Tann*, expecting an order to sortie any moment, had their torpedo nets lifted even before their relief by *Derfflinger* and *Seydlitz* around 8am. And instead of changing guard duty, all four vessels remained in deep water with steam up. But the expected order never came; instead, towards 10am, the battlecruisers were instructed to rig torpedo nets and stay in place. Soon after that the fog rolled over the Jade and out to sea, making operations impossible.

* Battle Squadrons IV, V and VI of the High Seas Fleet were organized at the start of the war for defensive duties. They were composed of old, obsolete ships that had been used for training or experimental purposes in peace-time, and were manned largely by reservists. The squadrons were disbanded before the end of 1916 and their ships disarmed for static harbour service.

The passivity of the Imperial Navy's surface forces was in sharp contrast to the active defence mounted immediately by its air arm, whose fliers were to prove equal to the British that day in skill and courage. The contrast deepens when it is recalled that the air branch, unlike the surface fleet, had apparently been given no warning that an enemy attack was likely.

As noted earlier, Zeppelin *L 6* had taken off from Nordholz for an armed reconnaissance over the bight even before the first reports of that attack were received, and was followed somewhat more than an hour later by *L 5*. At 7.50am, about the same time *L 5* was getting airborne, seaplanes from the Heligoland, Borkum and Sylt stations began taking off. The result of this prompt aerial response was the world's first high-seas aero-naval battle.

Unfortunately, it is impossible to give a coherent, totally accurate description of that battle; there are too many irreconcilable discrepancies in the British and German accounts of its events and their times. These differences are not to be wondered at, for it was a unique experience on both sides. Most of the German aviators were engaging surface ships for the first time, and the British seamen had never before been in action against aircraft. Men on both sides often literally did not know what they were seeing, and so more than the usual confusion and misconceptions cloud the accounts from which the story can be pieced together only partially.

As mentioned earlier, the Harwich Force was off Heligoland, having at 7.28am recovered the last of the two seaplanes unable to take off. Eight minutes later its look-outs spotted an airship about ten miles off, heading from the direction of the island. At 7.55am a seaplane was observed on the same bearing. Meanwhile, at 7.47 the squadron had shaped course to the south-west. This was the change of course seen by Lepsius through *U 6*'s periscope, and he thought it was dictated by the appearance of the airship.[1]

The ships spread into the formation ordered by Tyrwhitt for the route to Norderney. *Arethusa* and the eight destroyers were in line abreast, the cruiser at the centre with four destroyers on each flank. At a distance of 1½ cables behind the flagship came *Engadine*, with *Empress* abreast of her at five cables to port and *Riviera* in the same position to starboard. *Undaunted*, 1½ cables behind *Engadine*, brought up the rear.

Very soon, however, this formation was broken. Its 20-knot speed, close to the limit of *Engadine* and *Riviera*, was too much for *Empress*, which began to lag behind. She fell even farther back because of boiler room problems. She reportedly was suffering from condenser trouble,[2] but the great cause of her distress, according to Bowhill, was coal of inferior quality. To keep steam up, she had to burn this at such a high rate that the RNAS mechanics were pressed into service to assist the hard-shovelling stokers.[3]

The seaplane spotted from the ships at 7.55am was probably Friedrichshafen FF 19 No 80 from Heligoland. This plane immediately sped back to the island to deliver its contact report but must have made a second flight soon afterwards, for at 8.35, according to the German official history, the same aircraft observed two ships that its fliers mistakenly identified as *Talbot*-class cruisers lagging behind the main British formation, 'apparently with engine damage.'[4]

The airship seen by the British ten minutes earlier was *L 6*. This craft, commanded by Kapitänleutnant Horst Freiherr Treusch von Buttlar-Brandenfels, had steered for Heligoland after hearing radio reports of an enemy presence in the bight. At 7.30am an island searchlight flashed the message to the Zeppelin that the British force was to the north-east. Proceeding in that direction at 1600 feet, von Buttlar soon sighted the enemy ships and 'could clearly recognize their number, type, formation and course.'[5] But he was mystified by the carriers, which he described as 'steamers with funnels painted black'[6], and thought might be minelayers. A sighting report was prepared, but at this crucial moment the *L 6*'s radio generator broke down, leaving the Zeppelin unable to transmit for the rest of the day.

There ensued a baffling episode when von Buttlar steered north-west toward what appeared to be two ships detached from the main British formation – apparently the same vessels observed by seaplane No 80. What these craft may have been remains a mystery. There is no indication that any British vessels except *Empress* fell out of formation, and Tyrwhitt later reported that it was thought the seaplane and airship, while investigating the mystery ships, were circling over a British submarine.[7]

At any rate, it would seem that von Buttlar wasted an hour or more observing this peculiar contact before heading back for the British squadron at around 9am. By the time *L 6* had caught up with the Harwich Force the first German aerial attacks were being made.

The target was the laggard *Empress*, and the attackers were two seaplanes boring in from opposite sides of the ship. There is no doubt about the identity of the first plane. It was Friedrichshafen FF 19 No 26 from Heligoland and its fuselage number could be seen clearly as it swept over *Empress'* starboard bow at an estimated 2000 feet.

According to Bowhill's report, this plane dropped six bombs but 'made very bad shooting',[8] the missiles bursting 200 to 300 yards off the starboard bow. The German account states the plane dropped seven bombs from 1600 feet, and mistakenly credits it with three hits that started a fire on the ship.[9] Bowhill estimated the bombs as 10-pounders, which corresponds to the weight of the German 4.5-kilogram Carbonit missiles (very similar in principle to the Hale bombs) of 1914.

The second seaplane, coming in over the port bow moments later at an estimated 1800 feet, dropped two larger bombs, one exploding 20 feet off the port beam and shaking the ship, the other 40 feet from the starboard beam. Judging from the size of the bombs, this plane was probably Friedrichshafen FF 29 No 202, whose crew reported aiming two 10-kilogram (22-pound) bombs at a carrier.

To throw the planes' aim off, Bowhill 'continuously kept on altering my course'[10] in probably the first instance of a ship zig-zagging to avoid aerial attack. In the absence of a high-angle gun, *Empress* put up a barrage of anti-aircraft fire from rifles with which her crew seems to have been liberally supplied. Volleys were fired at the seaplanes while a few marksmen shot individually. None of this appeared to have any effect on the planes.

Now it was *L 6*'s turn. Von Buttlar caught up with the ships around 9.30am, flying through heavy clouds drifting in from the west that forced the Zeppelin below 1000 feet at times. Using one of these cloud formations to screen his approach, he arrived in time to see the finale of the seaplane attack. By dropping nearly all its water ballast, as well as three fuel tanks, *L 6* rose to 5500 feet and headed for *Empress*.

The British and German accounts diverge widely on what happened next. According to Bowhill, the airship, whose letter and number could be distinguished plainly, approached at 5000 feet from the starboard beam, than descended to 2000 feet and manoeuvred to get directly above the ship on a parallel course. 'She dropped two tracer bombs in order to obtain the range, and these were followed by three bombs of approximately 100 pounds each.'[11] The first exploded about 50 yards off the port quarter. The second and third fell 50 and 100 yards, respectively, astern and did not detonate.

According to von Buttlar, only one of his four 110-pound (50-kilogram) bombs was aimed at the ship and it missed by 100 to 160 feet. Since no times are given in either account, they cannot be reconciled. But it is possible that more time elapsed than Bowhill indicates between the dropping of the supposed 'tracer bombs' and the other three missiles. In that case, the 'tracer bombs' might have been the airship's falling water ballast* and the 'bombs' that did not explode two of its jettisoned fuel tanks.

Bowhill zig-zagged during this attack as he had against the seaplanes, aided by the fact that he could easily see the airship's ponderous rudders start to swing to follow the ship's course. Whenever he observed this, he would put the helm hard over in the opposite direction. The riflemen, meanwhile, banged away at *L 6*, and when the airship finally sheered off to the port quarter, the ship's aft 12-pounders were able to get off eight shots at it. Bowhill thought one shell-burst did some damage.

L 6 replied with fire from a machine gun positioned in its forward gondola. 'The shooting, however, was indifferent,' Bowhill reported,[12] and apparently not a single bullet struck *Empress*.

By now the carrier's plight was obvious to the other British ships, and *Undaunted* charged back to the rescue. She and *Arethusa* opened fire at the airship from 9000 to 11,000 yards range, using 6-inch shrapnel shell. 'Guns were at their extreme elevation and were consequently difficult to lay accurately.'[13] Nevertheless, *Undaunted* burst several shells uncomfortably close to *L 6* and this 'lively gunfire', as the German official history calls it,[14] caused von Buttlar to break off action and seek shelter in the clouds, dropping his remaining three bombs to help gain altitude.

With all bombs gone, still radioless, and now losing sight of the enemy, von Buttlar headed for Schillig Roads. There he descended low over armoured cruiser *Roon* and dropped a written report of his sightings and activities onto her quarterdeck, then steered for Nordholz, an hour's flight away. *L 6* landed, during one of the streaks of clear sky, at 12.30pm. Although the British believed that at least one of *Undaunted*'s shells had seriously damaged the Zeppelin, the airshipmen found only a handful of bullet holes in the gas cells – the work of *Empress*' riflemen.[15]

The Harwich Force reassembled after the attacks on *Empress* had been beaten off, allowing her to resume station from the position three miles behind, into which she had fallen, and apparently reducing speed to keep her in place this time. Soon after 9.30am the force turned south to reach the seaplane recovery position, and shortly before 10am *Fearless* and her eight destroyers were sighted, in perfect timing for their rendezvous. They manoeuvred to take station in the van.

* This phenomenon frequently baffled the British, who sometimes thought it was an attempt to lay a smoke screen.

As related in the previous chapter, by 9.30am or thereabouts, six of the seven British seaplanes, straggling back one by one after their unproductive raid, had reached Norderney and were heading seaward to find their floating bases. Their blind search in the fog for the airship base had brought four of them close to or even beyond their three-hour fuel limit, and gasoline gauges were hovering at, or precariously near, the empty mark. For these planes, the chances of reaching the carriers were slim.

The first pilot to find himself in this predicament was Ross in Short No 119. With fuel for only a few minutes longer, he sighted destroyers *Lurcher* and *Firedrake* 10 miles north of the Norderney Gat at 9.10am. He landed, taxied up to *Lurcher* and was taken aboard, where Keyes recognized him as the pilot with whom he had once flown during a prewar experiment in aerial detection of submarines.[16] *Lurcher* took the seaplane in tow, broke radio silence to inform Tyrwhitt of the recovery, and at 9.30 headed north. She met the Harwich Force an hour later, handed over Ross and the Short to *Engadine*, and steered back for Norderney. During the haul north she had sighted two British seaplanes and one German going the same direction.

The German plane probably was from the Borkum air base. The Britons were No 136, with Kilner and Childers, and Edmonds' No 811. No 136's navigation was perfect, but its engine trouble worsened seriously, the entire rear row of cylinders going out soon after the plane passed over *Lurcher* and *Firedrake*. Kilner nursed the sputtering craft to a landing near *Riviera* and it was hoisted aboard at 10.15am. Within five minutes Edmonds also reached the carrier, and thanks to the calm sea *Riviera* had to heave-to for no more than ten minutes to recover both planes. Robertson's decision that *Riviera*'s planes should be fuelled for a four-hour flight was now vindicated, for Nos 136 and 811 were the only aircraft to make it back to the carriers under their own power.

Soon after the three planes had been recovered the squadron came under new aerial attack. Once again there are wide discrepancies between the British and German descriptions. According to Tyrwhitt, 'several hostile seaplanes ... approached from the southward: all dropped bombs without success'[17] although 'several destroyers had narrow escapes.'[18] The German official history, however, indicates that only two seaplanes attacked – probably Friedrichshafen FF 19s No 25, the same plane that had tried to bomb *Liverpool* in November, and No 84.

No 25, flown by the commander of the Heligoland air station, Kapitänleutnant Berthold, aimed five bombs at destroyers and a cruiser. Berthold mistakenly claimed two hits. No 84 dropped two 10-kilogram bombs at a target identified as a cruiser.[19] The British may have magnified these two planes into 'several' because they were seen and logged at different times, positions and altitudes by various ships: the same sort of confusion had led the Germans to exaggerate the number of British seaplanes earlier in the day.

The carriers were ignored in this attack, and whatever the Germans' targets were, all ships came through unscathed. The British put up what seems to have been a considerable barrage from cannon (including anti-aircraft guns), machine guns and rifles. Tyrwhitt's November wish to see 'aerial' guns in operation was now gratified, but he was not pleased at the result, 'The converted 6-pounder anti-aircraft gun is not a success; the difficulty in training and want of tracer shell was very evident.'[20]

The British anti-aircraft fire, however, was not totally futile. Friedrichshafen No 25 was badly holed in the wings and at least one float, and when Berthold landed back at Heligoland the plane 'collapsed entirely'[21] and was a total loss. This was the only material success of the day for the British.

As the guns fell silent and the German seaplanes disappeared, Tyrwhitt ordered a jaunty signal run up *Arethusa*'s halyards: 'I wish all ships a merry Christmas.'

Although the three-hour deadline imposed by aircraft fuel capacity was now past, Tyrwhitt determined to wait a while longer in hope that the four overdue planes might yet appear. Unknown to him as he manoeuvred his force in various courses 20 to 30 miles off the coast, three of the errant ones had already ended their flights in the waters near Norderney.

At 9.30am submarine *E 11* was submerged in her assigned position six miles north-east of Norderney Gat when her skipper, Lieutenant Commander Martin E Nasmith,* spotted a seaplane through the periscope. Although the plane was at 1200 feet, Nasmith could identify it as British, and he ordered *E 11* to surface.

The plane was Miley's No 120. Its fuel was nearly exhausted and Miley could see no sign of the carriers ahead although the visibility was excellent. He sighted *E 11*'s periscope about the same time Nasmith saw the plane, and, as the submarine broke water, identified it as friendly by the red and white conning tower band. He landed alongside and asked the direction and distance

---

* Later Rear Admiral Sir Martin E Dunbar-Nasmith. He won fame and the Victoria Cross for his exploits with *E 11* in the Dardanelles and Sea of Marmara in 1915, and was commanding admiral of British submarines in 1929-31.

of the carriers. Told they were 25 miles away, Miley decided, since he had fuel for no more than five to ten minutes, to ask for a tow north.

Nasmith agreed. Miley went aboard *E 11*, taking his bombsight with him, and the Short was placed under tow at 9.50am. Ten minutes later *E 11*'s look-outs spotted an airship to starboard, approaching from the east. Almost at the same time a submarine was seen astern, on the surface and approaching *E 11* bow on so that identification was impossible. To top matters, moments later two British seaplanes appeared.

The first of these was No 814 with Gaskell Blackburn and Bell. They had passed *E 11* with No 120 in tow a few minutes earlier and had turned back to the submarine after failing to sight the Harwich Force to the north despite perfect visibility. 'My petrol being nearly finished,' Gaskell Blackburn reported, 'having been in the air 3 hours and 20 minutes, I landed near the submarine.'[22] The damaged float strut collapsed as he taxied toward *E 11* and the Short pitched nose down, rearing its tail into the air but remaining afloat.

No 814 was followed down almost immediately by No 815, with Oliver and Budds. They, too, were running dangerously low on fuel and had been unable to sight the carriers. After spotting *E 11*, Oliver 'decided to abandon machine owing to shortage of petrol, and landed near submarine.'[23]

No sooner had the two planes landed than the submarine astern was seen to dive, and Nasmith naturally interpreted this as the action of an enemy boat submerging to attack. This mysterious craft was in fact British *D 6*, *E 11*'s northern neighbour in the picket line of submarines. Her skipper, Lieutenant Commander R C Halahan (interestingly enough, a qualified aviator*), had seen the British planes preparing to land near *E 11* and was coming to assist when the close approach of the airship caused him to dive.

* This was not as unusual as it might seem. Flying and submarining had a similar appeal to young officers of many navies in the early twentieth century, both offering excitement, new and fascinating technology, and greater independence from rigid discipline. Besides Halahan (who was lost aboard *E 18* in the Baltic in 1916), other British submarine officers who took up flying privately were Lieutenant Commander C Head (lost when *D 2* was sunk in the North Sea just one month before the Cuxhaven Raid), Lieutenant (later RAF Group Captain) Hugh A Williamson, who transferred to the RNAS, becoming executive officer of *Ark Royal* during her Dardanelles service and later an unsung pioneer of the flightdeck carrier, and Lieutenant (later RAF Group Captain) Reginald J Bone, the *Empress* pilot who failed to take off on 25 December 1914. Bone's transfer to the RNAS from the submarine service was greatly to Keyes' dislike; according to Bone, Keyes held a grudge against him for years because of this.

The aerial craft was *L 5*, commanded by Kapitänleutnant Klaus Hirsch. After taking off from Nordholz about two hours earlier, it had followed *L 6* over the Weser, where at 7.12am it had seen three of the British seaplanes heading inland and radioed a report of them to its base. Sighting nothing to seaward, Hirsch had steered south-west and during his ship's progress along the coast it had been seen by Hewlett, Miley, Oliver and Gaskell Blackburn. All mistakenly reported it as a Schütte-Lanz.

Hirsch, however, apparently did not sight any of the planes that saw *L 5*, and when he spotted the three seaplanes clustered around *E 11*, rather naively assumed these were the same three he had seen earlier over the Weser.[24] There are no indications that *D 6* was seen from the airship, although Halahan thought it was heading for him, but the ships of the Harwich Force far to the north were visible to *L 5*'s crewmen.

Nasmith, tackling the problem of rescuing four airmen in the face of what appeared to be imminent underwater and aerial attack, acted with the cool-headed precision that would win him fame later in the war. Casting off the tow-line to No 120, he manoeuvred *E 11* so close to No 815 the Oliver and Budds were able to step aboard her, then hailed Gaskell Blackburn and Bell to swim to the submarine. Doffing their flying clothes and the impedimenta that Malone had insisted upon, they dived from their tilting plane and were hauled, dripping, aboard *E 11*.

Although the airship was now closing fast, Nasmith was obedient to the orders to destroy abandoned aircraft if possible. Since *E 11*, like most British submarines in 1914, as yet lacked a deck gun, he ordered a machine gun up from below and began to pepper the seaplanes' floats with it. Oliver joined in with his pistol.

Before this fire could have any effect, the aerial menace got too close for comfort, and Nasmith ordered a crash dive. With *L 5* nearly overhead, he waved his cap defiantly at it as he made for the conning tower hatch. It has often been claimed that this gesture confused the airshipmen into thinking *E 11* was a U-boat capturing enemy planes and caused them to delay dropping bombs. Gaskell Blackburn thought so at the time. But there is nothing in German accounts to suggest the gesture was even seen, and Hirsch's report makes it clear he was quite aware that the submarine was an enemy craft.[25] He saw the rescue of the airmen clearly just before he sent two bombs crashing down. Their explosions shook both *E 11* and *D 6*, although the former had time to dive to 40 feet before they went off and the latter was 60 feet down. The men on each submarine thought their boat was the airship's target, but Hirsch's account indicates he was aiming simply in the general vicinity of the seaplanes and the submerged *E 11*, hoping any or all might be damaged. Observing no effect from the bombs, he headed seaward toward the Harwich Force.

Nasmith meanwhile took *E 11* down to rest on the seabed, where at 20 fathoms the submariners shared their Christmas turkey and plum pudding with their five unusual guests.

Besides the seaplanes that attacked the British ships, others took to the air that morning to perform the less spectacular but essential task of reconnaissance. They carried out a thorough search of the bight, ranging to the south-west as far as the Dutch island of Terschelling in the West Frisian chain, seaward to the west out to the 5th meridian, and north up to the latitude of Esbjerg in Denmark.

Some of these flights were remarkable for distance and duration. Friedrichshafen FF 19 No 85 remained aloft for five hours and 52 minutes, a 'noteworthy achievement' indeed, as the German official history calls it, for a 1914 seaplane.[26] Albatros WWD No 24 at Heligoland, declared unserviceable the day before, was somehow coaxed into the air for a search stretching 100 miles west of the island. FF 19s, Nos 77 and 78 helped out with 'repeated flights.'[27]

The scouting planes spotted what they reported as British submarines north of Terschelling, at the mouth of the Ems, and 25 miles west of Sylt. The last was attacked by Albatros W1 No 53, which aimed two bombs at a submerged target heading south, with no observable effect. Whether this vessel was real or imaginary is not known. Conceivably, it could have been *E 6*, which had been assigned a patrol position near Heligoland and which, if submerged, could have been unaware of the attack. Or it might have been the unnamed submarine that Tyrwhitt reported was the target of six ineffective seaplane bombs.[28] Keyes, however, reports no such incident. The episode remains another of the mysteries of the Cuxhaven Raid.

This extensive early morning aerial reconnaissance, carried out while visibility was still excellent over the bight, plus the reports from the airships and the seaplanes that attacked the ships, soon gave the German naval command a reasonably accurate picture of what was going on at sea, although the seaplane reports were delayed by their lack of radio. By 10am it was clear that a

> group of light cruisers and destroyers with a few aircraft carriers ... had, while it was still dark, steered toward the Amrun shoal, had sent out aircraft there as it grew light, and then steered south-west in a

wide bend which ... avoided the mine-dangerous area at Heligoland, in order to await the return of the aircraft 20 nautical miles north of Borkum.[29]

It was also clear from the aerial scouting that there was no British supporting force anywhere in the bight, that the audacious little enemy formation would have been at the mercy of the High Seas Fleet had that fleet acted with less pusillanimity. Now it was too late; well before noon the fog had grown so thick and extensive over the northern estuaries that the overwhelmingly superior German strength was immobilized.

There remained the possibility of acting against the British intruders with the submarines stationed in the Ems, which was still clear although the fog was beginning to creep in. At 10.10am, at the urging of Korvettenkapitän Hermann Bauer, commander of the submarine service, the naval authorities ordered submarine Half-Flotilla III at Emden to send two boats to occupy positions astride the assumed line of retreat of the British force in hopes of intercepting it. They were to remain there until the following day on the chance that the aerial pinprick had been only a prelude to a major attack the next morning, an attack whose line of advance might take it within range of the lurking U-boats. One submarine was already near the assigned positions – *U 20*, one of the two ordered out the previous day, lying north of Norderney. She was commanded by Kapitänleutnant Walter Schweiger, who would gain world-wide notoriety five months later when, still skipper of *U 20*, he sank the liner *Lusitania*.

Korvettenkapitän Albert Gayer, commander of Half-Flotilla III, had acted independently and energetically long before the high command bestirred itself. Immediately after the first reports of the British attack were received, he had ordered *U 30* to relieve *U 20*, *U 19* at Emden to prepare to sail, *U 32* to stand by, and *U 22* to advance at highest possible speed 55 miles north to intercept the enemy force on its probable line of withdrawal. Then he pushed out to sea himself on the half-flotilla flagship, the old destroyer *T 100*, for a personal reconnaissance.

Gayer was at sea when the order from headquarters was received, in garbled form, to station his boats for interception, with another position added to the two originally determined. Unwilling to break radio silence at sea, Gayer returned to the Ems and by searchlight ordered the waiting *U 32* to take up the second of these positions. Some time after this, *U 19* signalled from Emden that the fog was now too thick for her to sail. Gayer ordered her out regardless, but apparently because of difficulty in navigating in the fog she did not arrive off Borkum until 4pm.

The first submarine brush with the British had occurred even as Gayer was taking action early in the morning. At 8.15am Schweiger sighted two destroyers, without doubt *Lurcher* and *Firedrake*, four miles distant in line ahead, steering east. The foremost appeared to be signalling with a searchlight to a submarine (probably *E 11*) to the westward, which then submerged while the destroyers headed north. Then smoke was sighted to the north; Schweiger headed for it and at 10.45am spotted a four-funnelled cruiser and eight destroyers steaming in line abreast. It was *Fearless* and her First Flotilla brood, cruising in advance of Tyrwhitt. They had already been sighted by *U 22* at 10.25 after the U-boat had glimpsed a British submarine, and at 11 were seen by *U 30*.

Tyrwhitt's cruiser/destroyer/carrier force was spotted by *U 22* at 11.32 and by *U 30* at 11.45. *U 30* noted an airship that seemed to be pursuing this force, and *U 22* distinguished the three carriers, assuming them to be minelayers.

Between 10.45am and 12.15pm all three submarines attempted to attack the enemy ships at various times, but were repeatedly frustrated by the Britons' rapid and frequent changes of course and formation, and by the thick smoke the surface ships were making. *U 20* was able to get within 1000 yards of a prospective target only once. Close on noon the entire British force was seen to turn west amd make off at high speed. *U 20* retired toward the Ems and radioed a report of the enemy withdrawal.

U 22 lost sight of the British at 12.15pm and continued northward, sighting an apparent enemy submarine at 2.25pm. She did not attack, although in a favourable firing position, because there was no way to adjust the depth settings of her torpedoes for the shallow draft of a submarine while they were in their tubes. At 3.27 she surfaced and returned to the Ems, and later went to the sea bottom for the night.

Gayer ordered *U 20* northward again to take up a waiting position until the next evening. She went to ground at 7pm.

U 32, although delayed in the western channel of the Ems by what her captain thought was a torpedo attack by an enemy submarine, crossed the British line of retreat too soon and sighted nothing until 3.45pm, when a submarine was seen but not attacked because it could not be identified as enemy. She reached her assigned station and submerged to the sea bottom at 7.55.

U 30, which had relieved *U 20* off Borkum, was herself relieved by the delayed *U 19* the next morning. All submarines except *U 30* and another that had relieved *U 5* in the north-east returned to port that day and the next, after it was apparent that no further enemy action could be expected.[30]

Although, thanks to Gayer, the Imperial Navy's submarine service had responded as promptly and energetically as its aerial arm, it had been equally ineffective in its offensive action. The rapid, continual manoeuvring of the British force prevented a single U-boat from reaching a position to launch torpedoes.

Were the British aware they were being stalked underwater? Superficially, it would seem so. 'Several submarines were seen,' Tyrwhitt reported, 'and both *Arethusa* and *Fearless* were attacked without success; high speed and rapid use of the helm having the desired effect.'[31] Keyes wrote

> Several hostile submarines were sighted. The duties of our sub-marines kept them on the surface a good deal, and ... at least four unsuccessful attacks were delivered on them by hostile submarines. There were apparently avoided before the enemy could manoeuvre into position to fire.[32]

However, by December of 1914 the Royal Navy was so sensitive to and conscious of the submarine menace that any movement by it in the North Sea was inevitably accompanied by a rash of U-boat 'sightings' and 'attacks', a condition that continued through the war. The vast majority of these were false alarms – floating debris or reflections on the waves translated into periscopes and torpedo tracks by the imagination of nervous, keyed-up look-outs. It is difficult to believe that this kind of delusion did not occur aboard the Harwich Force ships on 25 December. As for the 'attacks' reported by Tyrwhitt, they must have been defined as Keyes defined 'attacks' on his submarines, when a submarine was said to 'attack' whether or not it actually fired a torpedo.

In any event, it has become a legend of the Cuxhaven Raid that the Harwich Force fended off a number of submarines while waiting for the seaplanes' return, and in this case the legend is true.

The airship that *U 30*'s captain thought was 'pursuing' the British force was *L 5*. At its high altitude, it had been visible from Tyrwhitt's ships and to Keyes on *Lurcher* during its approach toward *E 11* and the downed seaplanes. After that submarine had disappeared underwater, Hirsch steered the Zeppelin toward the British squadron as it manoeuvred against the U-boats while still waiting vainly for its remaining planes.

Keeping a respectful distance, Hirsch followed the ships as they steamed alternate southern, eastern and western courses. Whenever this circular manoeuvring brought *L 5* southward, it

The Cuxhaven Raid

would descend and take the three derelict seaplanes under machine-gun fire. During one of these intervals, Halahan, unaware that the aviators had already been rescued, brought *D 6* to the surface to offer assistance to the supposedly marooned fliers. Thinking one burst of machine-gun fire from *L 5* was directed at his boat, he immediately dived again, but not before he had found the planes abandoned.

Aboard *Arethusa*, Tyrwhitt began to think about retirement. It had been nearly five hours since the planes took off, and 'It was now painfully evident that the remaining four seaplanes were not likely to be in the air.'[33] After making one last sweep in the direction of Norderney, at 11.45am he reluctantly signalled for course to be shaped for west-north-west and home. The withdrawal was observed by *U 20* and *U 22* below the waves and *L 5* above them. The airship followed for a while, but a fog had begun to rise to seaward and at 12.15pm Hirsch lost sight of the ships in the mist and turned back.

The return flight took *L 5* over the three British seaplanes again, and Hirsch descended to inspect them more closely and leisurely than before. Their identification numbers and insignia were clearly visible. Hirsch radioed a report of their position and continued back to Nordholz.

There are several conflicting versions of the final fate of these planes. According to the German official history, the fog soon became too dense for their recovery to be attempted,[34] but another German account says one was salvaged and towed to Heligoland, where it was, inexplicably, identified as an Avro.[35] Miley stated that his No 120 was destroyed by machine-gun fire from *L 5* – which he, Tyrwhitt, Keyes and several others misidentified as a Schütte-Lanz – after it had drifted into what for no discernable reason he thought was a minefield. Keyes reported ambiguously that Halahan, who brought *D 6* up again after *L 5* had finally left, 'satisfied himself that all three seaplanes had been sunk.'[36] It is apparently on the basis of this statement that many accounts say Halahan himself sank the planes, which he would have had to do by ramming, since *D 6* had no deck gun. It is more probable that Keyes meant what other versions have said: that Halahan was unable to sight the planes again and therefore presumed they had gone down. It can only be assumed that somewhere, sometime, the North Sea swallowed the three gallant little craft.

The Harwich Force headed homeward, at 16¼ knots in deference to the limping *Empress* and also to *Riviera*, which was

110

having difficulty in making as much as 18 knots 'owing to the fires becoming dirty'.[37] Only two British surface ships remained on the scene, Keyes' *Lurcher* and *Firedrake*. Keyes had stood back toward Norderney Gat after handing over the seaplane to *Engadine*, and somewhat more than an hour later was 'much relieved' by Tyrwhitt's withdrawal, 'as it seemed incredible that strong enemy forces were not on their way to attack [the carriers].'[38] After that he headed for the Ems and Terschelling, appointing *Lurcher* and *Firedrake* a two-ship task force 'to prevent the enemy's torpedo craft and trawlers from interfering with our submarines returning on the surface.'[39]

At 2.30pm *Lurcher* received a radio report from *E 11*, which was running homeward on the surface after her underwater Christmas party, of the rescue of the five airmen. Thirty minutes later a German seaplane approached the destroyer from astern, so low that it was well within the angle of elevation of the aft 4-inch gun. Keyes, standing near the gunlayer, 'told him to give his gun a swing up as he fired, as one does for a rocketing pheasant.'[40] The gun barked off a single shot and the seaplane 'twisted and turned like a pigeon … and like a pigeon flew away.'[41] This was probably the plane (most likely flying from Borkum), that at 4pm, after the final German reconnaissance flight of the day, reported an enemy destroyer the airmen thought was the last British ship making its withdrawal.[42]

Actually, Keyes stayed until nightfall patrolling between the Ems and Terschelling. Finally, after having sighted nothing in five hours, he headed for Harwich at 8pm; 'so ended a most memorable Christmas Day.'[43]

The submarines followed, all returning without incident on 26 and 27 December. Except for *E 11* and *D 6*, their stay in German waters had been uneventful. Not one had found a target for its torpedoes, thanks to German inactivity (*U 32*'s report of a torpedo attack on it was incorrect). A few of them had spotted some of the German submarines, but the only enemy surface ship sighted during the entire operation was a vessel seen by *E 7* south of Heligoland, thought to be a destroyer, heading away from the main British squadron.

The Harwich Force's return passage was as uneventful as its outward-bound voyage had been, but all hands from Tyrwhitt down who knew that six airmen were missing were depressed by the apparent loss. The mood was brightened when the return of *Lurcher* brought the news that five of the lost were safe and sound.

But Hewlett's fate was still unknown, and it was assumed during the next five days that the supposed British seaplane seen in the water between Heligoland and the mainland soon after take-off had been his. The presumed death or capture of this popular and well-liked officer was much mourned.

Whatever the mysterious plane may have been, however, it was not Hewlett's, for he was still in the air nearly three hours later. We left him just after 9am on the 25th, flying north in a vain attempt to find the carriers. He ended up furthest afield of all the pilots; exactly where is impossible to say, for his report gives no indication of navigational positions, probably because he did not know them. It would appear, however, that he had overshot the Frisian chain entirely when at 9.25am the Short's engine began to misfire, lose power, and overheat from lack of oil.

It was obvious that he would have to land soon. Fortunately, there was a small trawler in sight and he circled around it to determine its nationality: 'Seeing that she flew the Dutch flag, I landed by her, secured astern, and asked the captain if he could give me any oil.'[44] The answer was no, so Hewlett waited for two hours in the hope a British ship might appear. When none did, he tried to restart the engine, but it was now hopelessly seized up. The trouble, he discovered, had been caused by a misadjustment of the device governing oil distribution, although he had checked it earlier and given his mechanic instructions on the proper setting.

When no ship had been sighted by nightfall, Hewlett punched and shot holes in the plane's floats and had it cast off. It was last seen sinking with only the tail visible.

For the better part of the following week, Hewlett remained aboard the trawler, the *Maria van Hattem*, while the Dutchmen hauled up their catches, unwilling to let a little thing like an aviator dropping from the blue interfere with serious business. On 31 December the vessel finally pulled into the North Holland port of Ymuiden (today IJmuiden), north-west of Amsterdam. There, Hewlett was greeted with glad cries by the British vice consul, who reported his arrival to the Admiralty that same day. His release was soon arranged under the pretext he was a 'shipwrecked mariner.' A precedent had been set for this in September, with the repatriation from the same port of crew members of the sunken cruiser *Hogue*, but Hewlett's release would seem to be the first use of a ploy that during the next three and a half years would spare many British fliers from internment in Holland. He arrived back in England on 3 January.[45] Writing his official report that day, he concluded: 'I deeply regret that I

should have caused so much trouble and should have necessi-
tated the loss of a seaplane to the Naval Air Service.'[46]

The final act of the Cuxhaven Raid drama was played out many
miles away in the middle of the North Sea. The elements of the
Grand Fleet had rendezvoused there by 1.20pm on the 25th and
headed south-south-east at 15 knots. For the rest of the day the
fleet steered various courses, never approaching within 100 miles
of Heligoland. The light cruisers *Birmingham* and *Southampton*
reported sighting submarines. Toward evening the sea began to
rise, and by 9.15pm was so heavy that speed had to be reduced to
permit the destroyers to keep up.

The morning of 26 December found the Battle Fleet at 50°58'
north latitude, 2°16' east longitude, with the battlecruisers 40
miles to the south. The weather was still deteriorating, and at
8.10am the destroyers had to be detached to return to their bases.
By 10am a full gale was howling, with mountainous waves, and
Jellicoe ordered the sweep abandoned, turning north and
dispersing the various squadrons to head for their bases: 'Bad
weather continued during the passage north, with a very rough
sea.'[47] Three men were lost overboard from destroyers of the
Second Flotilla, and one was washed from the light cruiser
Caroline. These would seem to be the only casualties suffered by
either side during all the operations of the Cuxhaven Raid.

The destroyers were badly buffeted during the return voyage;
three of them, *Hope*, *Redpole* and *Ruby*, were so heavily damaged
they required dockyard repair.

Worse was to follow as the Battle Fleet started to enter Scapa
Flow during the pre-dawn hours of 27 December in heaving seas
and with a following wind that blew funnel smoke over bridges.
The battleship *Conqueror* of the Second Battle Squadron collided
with the ship ahead, *Monarch*, which had stopped to avoid a
patrol trawler. *Monarch*'s stern and *Conqueror*'s starboard bow
were severely damaged.

There was a lingering sequel to this accident. *Monarch* was
patched up sufficiently to allow her to sail on 29 December for
complete repair at Devonport, but *Conqueror* was in worse shape.
It took the combined efforts of the fleet repair ship *Assitance* plus
the salvage ship *Rattler*, specially sent from Liverpool, before she
could leave for permanent repair. Even then, the seas were too
heavy for her when she sailed on 21 January, and she had to turn
back for more work. Finally, made temporarily seaworthy, she
reached Invergordon on 24 January and underwent more repair
in the floating drydock there before being able to proceed to

Liverpool for complete patching up by Cammel Laird & Co.

Monarch, meanwhile, rejoined the fleet on 20 January, but *Conqueror* did not return to Scapa Flow until 6 March. The absence of these two vessels and the loss of *Audacious* to a mine in October, meant that for a time, the strength of the Second Battle Squadron was reduced to five ships.

The storm that had started on Christmas Day raged across the northern North Sea during the last week of 1914, immobilizing ships and aircraft of the rival fleets. On 29 December the storm accomplished what the British had been unable to – a south-easterly gale tore off a portion of the Nordholz hangar's roof and a falling beam pierced a gas cell in *L 5*. Luckily, there were no chance sparks to touch off a fire, and the cell was repaired and refilled. That night the hangar had to be turned four times, as the wind shifted, to prevent further damage.[48]

The weather, which had influenced and shaped the events and outcome of the Cuxhaven Raid far more than the plans and attempts of man, had had the final word.

Short No 136 shown being hoisted out of the water. *By courtesy of P H Liddle via G S Leslie*

CHAPTER 9

The Daring of the Attempt

A fter the Great War, when historians came to puzzle out what had happened where and when, the struggles of that conflict were given names to put them into chronological or geographical context. Some names stuck, some did not. Thus the great clash of the British and German fleets in 1916 finally came to be known to the English-speaking world as Jutland after the name first attached to it by Jellicoe, but the names of the eight stages into which the official historians divided the protracted British agony on the Somme in 1916 have been almost entirely forgotten, and the officially titled Third Battle of Ypres is far better known as Paschendaele.

The Cuxhaven Raid was never given a battle name, for, by contemporary standards, it was not a battle. It was called 'The Air Raid on Cuxhaven' in the popular press of the time and later when official documents relating to the raid were assembled 'Seaplane Operations Against Cuxhaven', but eventually became known simply as 'The Cuxhaven Raid'.

But it was in fact a battle, the first of a kind that would become familiar in the next war, and it is fair to apply to it the criteria of a battle in trying to determine who won, who lost, what was achieved, and what the consequences were.

Under the criterion of material loss, the British were certainly the worse sufferers. Although it would appear that the four men lost at sea were the Royal Navy's only casualties, it sustained the loss of four seaplanes, the disablement of two battleships (one for 3½ weeks, one for 10 weeks) and the more temporary disablement of three destroyers and a submarine. The Germans lost one seaplane and sustained slight to trival damage to an airship, a trawler and possibly one or two seaplanes.

Moreover, the British failed entirely in their objective. The Nordholz airship base was not only not attacked, it was not even located. This failure was so complete that Malone was moved to comment, 'It is possible that the airship sheds supposed to be in the vicinity of Cuxhaven are non-existent.'[1]

How much damage was done by the British planes? No great claim was made at the time. The official public statement on the raid released by the Secretary of the Admiralty said, 'The extent of the damage by the British airmen's bombs cannot be estimated, but all were discharged on points of military significance.'[2] A greatly inflated estimate, however, was soon in Admiralty hands. There is no clue to its source, but it almost certainly came from secret agents. According to this report 'extensive damage' was done, including damage to 'a revolving aircraft shed ... a number of houses and a section of the quay' and 'coast forts and gasworks.'[3] It continued to say that two colliers had been sunk and the destroyer G 170 'struck abaft the mainmast,' while casualties numbered 67 seamen and 12 civilians killed, 11 seamen and 36 civilians wounded.[4]

This was sheer fantasy, and if the report did come from spies they were probably deluded by exaggerated lower deck rumour, such as the story circulating on one German battleship immediately after the raid that a cruiser and another vessel had been hit and a large fire started.[5] It is doubtful that the Admiralty placed much credence in these claims, for they were apparently never made public, although Sueter repeated some of them in 1928 in his book *Airmen or Noahs*.[6]

Official British postwar claims were vague and relatively modest. The official naval history stated that bombs were dropped 'apparently with effect, though the damage done was variously reported,'[7] and the air history merely claimed 'a good deal of damage was done by bomb-dropping.'[8] Neither attempted to give any details. Since then many writers have used their imaginations to fill in the blanks.

The fact is that the British never did know what the bombing accomplished, and apparently never really tried to find out. The Germans, being on the receiving end, did know, and in a radio message soon after the raid – it seems to have been a public communiqué – stated the seaplanes 'threw bombs at an anchored ship and a gasometer in the vicinity of Cuxhaven without hitting them or causing any damage.'[9] This seems a very accurate summary of the only bomb-dropping of any consequence, although incorrectly assuming the incident at Nordholz was a deliberate attack. These two bombings (at Nordholz and Edmonds' attack on *Stralsund* and *Graudenz*) are also the only ones mentioned in the German official naval history.

There is no mention in German sources of the bombs dropped

Table II

Distribution of Bombs in Cuxhaven Raid

Aircraft number	Number of bombs	Location	Supposed Target	Actual Target
119	1	Near Wangeroog island	Submerged submarine	Unknown
815	3	Langeoog island	Seaplane base	Unknown; probably sheds or warehouse
811	3	Weser estuary	Two cruisers	Cruisers *Stralsund* and *Graudenz*
814	2	Near Wilhelmshaven	Land battery	Unknown
814	1	Near Wilhelmshaven	City of Wilhelmshaven	Unknown

by Oliver at the imaginary seaplane base on Langeoog, reinforcing the supposition that if he did hit anything it was an inconsequential civilian structure.

Difficult as it is to make an accurate appraisal nearly three-quarters of a century later, it would seem nearly certain that the 10 bombs dropped all fell harmlessly on woods, fields, dunes or water, inflicting no military damage of any kind. (See Table II for a summary of the bombing.)

The reconnaissance aspects of the operation were carried out somewhat more successfully, especially by Kilner and Childers, who turned in the most useful report. But the fog prevented their obtaining hard-and-fast answers to some of the Admiralty's questions. The negative information was gained that there appeared to be no swept channel leading to the Jade, no boom defending Schillig Roads, and no worthwhile shore targets near the roadstead. It could not be judged how many Elbe lightvessels were still in place. Childers was able to plot some of the anchorages in Schillig Roads, but none of the fliers scouted Wilhelmshaven.

It has been claimed that an indirect effect of the raid was to cause the High Seas Fleet to send some units into the Kiel Canal and the Baltic until anti-aircraft defences could be strengthened. There is no truth to this report, which apparently was based on observation of the fact that ships of the German battle fleet frequently sheltered in the canal locks, and the starting in October divisions or squadrons were sometimes sent into the Baltic for manoeuvres or gunnery practice. Battle Squadron III went to the Baltic for this purpose in late January, and it may have been that this transit, which was reported by British spies in Wilhelm-shaven and Kiel, was interpreted as a response to the air raid.

Another supposed indirect consequence of the Cuxhaven Raid has grown into an enduring myth. It is the story that the appearance of the British planes over the Jade caused the German ships there to up-anchor hurriedly in consternation and dismay, and that in the confusion the battlecruiser *Von der Tann* collided with another vessel and was severely damaged. This, it is said, was the reason *Von der Tann* was not present at the Battle of the Dogger Bank four weeks later; instead the armoured cruiser *Blücher* was substituted for the damaged ship, and thus the air raid was indirectly responsible for the sinking of the *Blücher* in that battle.*

This thesis was stated as absolute fact in the British naval history,[10] its credence was reinforced by other postwar writings, and it has been repeated by nearly everyone who has written about the Cuxhaven Raid in the English language during the past five decades. Sometimes *Moltke* is identified as the other vessel in the supposed collision, probably on the basis of a statement by Keyes in his memoirs.[11] Actually, nothing of the kind happened. The German official historian took pains to deny it, rather testily.[12] But is spite of this denial and in the face of clear-cut evidence of its non-occurance, the myth persists.

The story's origin did not stem from the Cuxhaven Raid itself, for none of the British airmen reported seeing such an incident. Instead, British documents reveal that its source was statements made by prisoners from the sunken *Blücher*.[13] These men may have been deliberately lying to their captors, but since they would have had nothing to gain from such a fabrication, it seems unlikely. It is more probable they were simply repeating lower deck scuttlebutt.

The truth is that *Blücher* had already been attached to Scouting Squadron I and had participated in the November and December operations against the English coast. She did not, therefore, replace *Von der Tann* in the operation leading to the Dogger Bank battle, but would have been present anyhow. *Von der Tann* was

---

* Rear Admiral Franz von Hipper, commander of Scouting Group I, has been almost universally criticized for incorporating the *Blücher* into his squadron, on the basis that she was inferior to both German and British battlecruisers in firepower and speed, thus making her loss nearly inevitable. Actually, under the conditions of Dogger Bank she was able to maintain squadron speed, and her guns, although lighter calibre than those of the German battlecruisers, had a longer range. See Tobias R Philbin, *Admiral von Hipper: The Inconvenient Hero* (B R Gruner, Amsterdam: 1982), pp. 108-111.

Short No 136 shown here in Kephalo Bay, the Dardanelles in April 1915. Cecil F Kilner piloted this seaplane in the Cuxhaven Raid. It was flown safely through a barrage of fire from German battlecruisers and battleships as it headed towards the Schillig Roads, escaping with slight damage. *By courtesy of G R Bromet via G S Leslie*

On the left Cecil F Kilner. He flew Short Type 135 No 136, with Robert Erskine Childers as his observer. Although their flight in the Cuxhaven Raid was not successful as a bombing mission, they made the most important observations of the day. *Fleet Air Arm Museum*

not present only because of a quirk in the weather and the demands of routine maintenance. She was scheduled to take part in a battlecruiser raid set for 21 January, but the weather became so bad that the operation was called off. After the cancellation, *Von der Tann* was ordered into drydock for a 12-day routine overhaul. She entered the Wilhelmshaven dockyard on the morning of 23 January. That afternoon there was a sudden improvement in weather and the cancelled operation was immediately rescheduled, although with a change of direction and aim. But it was too late for *Von der Tann* to rejoin Scouting Squadron I when its ships sailed later that day in the sortie that resulted in the Dogger Bank action.[14]

Such are the facts, but they have been unable over the years to prevail against the pernicious endurance of a hoary legend of the Cuxhaven Raid.

It was, as we have seen, the British, not the German battle fleet that was weakened as a result of the Cuxhaven Raid. The long absence of the *Conqueror* was one of the factors, together with absence of other vessels for essential overhauls and the despatch of battlecruisers to deal with matters in distant waters, that brought the Grand Fleet to its lowest point of numerical superiority over the High Seas Fleet. For a while in January, Jellicoe and Beatty had only a one-ship advantage over their German opponents: 18 dreadnought battleships to 17, 5 battle-cruisers to 4.[15]

Here, for all practical purposes, was the battle line parity the Germans had sought, the goal of their guerrilla operations achieved, not by their exertions but by pure luck. It was perhaps the one time in the entire conflict when the German fleet, if handled with the tactical and technical skill it was to display at Jutland, could have dared a major action with a good chance of winning. It is the greatest paradox of the Cuxhaven Raid that this attempt to shield Britain against the new threat from the air caused the weakening of the surest, strongest element of her protection from the sea. But the Germans were unwilling or unable to exploit the opportunity they had unwittingly been given, and it would not occur again.

While there is no truth to the story the Cuxhaven Raid drove German fleet units away from their bases, it did result in strengthening of air defences ashore and afloat. The Nordholz base was assigned some medium- and light-calibre anti-aircraft guns, and the giant shed coated with dark paint to reduce its location-revealing reflection.[16] The raid probably gave impetus to continued equipping ships of the fleet with anti-aircraft weapons during the next few months.

The action at sea on the 25th impressed the British also with the need for more shipboard anti-aircraft artillery. Both the cruisers and the carriers had been handicapped by the lack of high-angle guns. Bowhill, although opining that 'a Zeppelin attack can be beaten off by a continuous rifle fire,'[17] believed that during *Empress'* action with *L 6* 'had an anti-aircraft gun been on board we could not have failed to bring her [*L 6*] down.'[18]

Malone also turned in a recommendation for more AA guns, and in early January, Churchill announced to the War Council that such guns were being placed on Royal Navy ships as expediently as possible. When *Engadine, Riviera* and *Empress* returned to service after their extensive remodelling in 1915 they sported high-angle guns, although they were the 6-pounders that Tyrwhitt had found so unsatisfactory.

The action also allayed British apprehension about the airship as a weapon at sea. The fabulous monster had finally been met, and had proved far less alarming than had been feared. Tyrwhitt found the Zeppelins 'ridiculously easy to avoid in spite of their speed'[19] and later referred to them as 'stupid great things'. Bowhill believed that a ship with anti-aircraft guns 'would always bring a Zeppelin down in daytime, should she attack.'[20] These opinions were probably over-optimistic, but they were never to be tested. Practically never during the rest of the war did airships approach a surface force so closely or again try to bomb moving warships on the open sea.

Tyrwhitt was more impressed with the seaplane attacks, which 'were of a much more active nature although they do not appear to have discovered the art of hitting.'[21] Malone also commented on the more accurate aim of the aeroplane bombs. But by and large, history's first naval-air battle saw the palms go to the surface ships. Tyrwhitt concluded from it 'that, given ordinary sea room, our ships have nothing to fear from seaplanes or Zeppelins.'[22] It was a conclusion valid for nearly the rest of the war.

And so, despite the failure of the raid in its primary purpose, the British had much to be pleased about. The air threat had been met and apparently mastered; the submarine air-rescue scheme (the forerunner of similar use of submarines by the American navy in the Pacific war) had worked well, and lessons had been learned for the future. One lesson was the excellence of the latest Short seaplanes, despite their engine problems. Robertson declared:

Photograph taken on the decks of *Engadine*. Sitting down: in the centre Arnold J Miley, on his left A B Gaskell and at the end Robert P Ross. Standing up, in the centre Squadron Commander Cecil J L'Estrange Malone, captain of *Engadine*,

commanding officer of the three seaplane carriers and in tactical command of the nine seaplanes. *Fleet Air Arm Museum*

the 200 hp Short No 136 appears to be the ideal machine for this work … this machine appears to stand out well above the other types used, and I strongly recommend that future machines of this type should be ordered and sent to the carrier.[23]

Probably unknown to him, Short Brothers' designers were already at work on the successor to No 136. It would emerge early the next year as the Admiralty Type 184 and would be a work-horse of British naval aviation for the rest of the war.

Significantly, the Short 184 was originally designed as a torpedo plane, and the experiences of the Cuxhaven Raid indicated to some of its participants the potential of that weapon. Malone wrote, 'One can well imagine what might have been done had our seaplanes, or those which were sent our to attack us, had carried torpedoes … Several of the ships in Schelling [Schillig] Roads would have been torpedoed and some of our force might have been sunk as well.'[24] This thought occurred as well to Edmonds, who later commented to Sueter that the German battlecruisers in the Jade would have made a splendid target for aerial torpedoes.[25] Seven months after the Cuxhaven Raid, Edmonds and Malone would carry out history's first aerial torpedo attacks, far from the North Sea.

Altogether, then, nearly every element of future naval war had coalesced in the Cuxhaven Raid in embryonic form. The most prescient appraisal was written by Malone: 'In conclusion, I look upon the events which took place on 25 December as a visible proof of the probable line in the development of the principles of naval strategy.'[26] History would fulfil his prediction.

There was another reason for British satisfaction with the raid, a greater one than the success of tactical innovations. This was the fact that, just as much as the 28 August operation, the 25 December attack established a British moral ascendancy. For approximately eight hours (4am to noon) a weak, unsupported force had cruised at will within 50 miles of the German coast without a riposte from the major elements of the High Seas Fleet. For at least half that time the position and composition of the British squadron were known accurately by the German naval command, as well as the significant fact that the intruders had no big-gun backing. Yet the only response to this impudent nose-thumbing was semi-independent action by the air and sub-surface forces.

The British were elated by the fact the High Seas Fleet failed to act until after 10am, by which time the fog had made action impossible. This failure has been noted in all subsequent accounts of the Cuxhaven Raid, and the High Seas Fleet has been the target of much criticism for it. This critical attitude has not been confined to British or pro-British writers. Captain Otto Groos, the first of the two German official historians of the North Sea war, caustically upbraided the naval command for its timidity and inaction.[27]

Why did the High Seas Fleet fail to act? Various reasons have been advanced, but none holds water. Groos suggests it was 'the expectation that the aircraft were merely harbingers of a larger enemy action,'[28] causing the naval command to withhold major units until the situation developed, plus over-apprehension about British submarines. Both these excuses are flimsy, especially the first since it was soon known that no 'larger attack' could possibly be in the offing. Groos notes, 'the conditions for … an immediate counterthrust, the moral importance of which could not have been underestimated … were particularly favourable on that day, before the fog set in.'[29] The most logical response, he feels, would have been action by the fully combat-ready battlecruisers and destroyers in the Jade, which 'could have attacked … almost immediately after receipt of the first reports.'[30]

From the German standpoint, the Cuxhaven Raid was, as Groos correctly assesses it, a 'minor attack' and 'a failure' on the tactical level. But in the moral sphere it was a resounding German defeat. The lethargy of the naval command in the face of a daring enemy venture was a harbinger of the attitude that would later keep the High Seas Fleet idle for months on end – months of morale-rotting boredom that would end just short of four years after the Cuxhaven Raid with the imperial flag replaced by the red banner of mutiny.

If the raid was a German moral defeat, it was equally a British moral victory. That it was a material failure was not really recognized at the time, and in fact to this day it is accounted as a victory by the Royal Navy and its air arm. For even when its lack of military success was realized, that fact was overwhelmed by the daring, courage and skill displayed. Tyrwhitt wrote of the aviators, 'I consider these officers, who carried out a 120-mile flight, deserve the highest credit and gave a magnificent exhibition of British pluck, daring and endurance.'[31]

The Admiralty was equally impressed and pleased. Tyrwhitt was given a 'most complimentary'[32] reception by the board, and on 6 January Sueter received a message expressing:

their Lordships' appreciation of the skilful [sic] arrangements made for the air reconnaissance of the Heligoland Bight and attack on military points at Cuxhaven ... and of the success with which that reconnaissance and attack were carried out. Their Lordships regard the work of the seaplane carriers and seaplanes in assisting to bring this novel and dangerous enterprise to a successful issue as having been exceptionally good.[33]

As the first large-scale *naval* operation of the Royal Naval Air Service, and the most daring feat of maritime flying yet in the war, the Cuxhaven Raid contributed much to the morale and tradition of that service. The tradition became an inspiring part of the annals of British aviation, cherished by succeeding RNAS fliers, and eventually, as many of those fliers entered the new national air service, came to occupy an honoured spot in the legacy of the Royal Air Force.

Had Wilhelm II given any thought to the events on the northern coast of his empire on 25 December 1914, he might well have pondered the words of Philip II after Francis Drake's descent upon Cadiz 327 years earlier: 'The loss was not very great, but the daring of the attempt was very great indeed.'

CHAPTER 10

Zeppelin, Flieg

It is most unlikely that the Kaiser did give any thought to the Cuxhaven Raid. On Christmas Day he motored from his headquarters at Charleville in occupied France to Douai, where he inspected a guards regiment and treated its men to one of his bombastic speeches.[1] Any report of the raid, even if one were given to him, must have been dismissed after a cursory glance.

Nor was the Kaiser aware that the game of *Luftpolitik* was still being played behind his back that day. Von Pohl was informed by the army that its airships were going to be sent on a strong raid against three cities in France; the message suggested the navy Zeppelins co-operate. At the same time, he received a message from Strasser saying the weather was favourable for aerial operations against England. In a moment of weakness, von Pohl succumbed to temptation and gave permission for a raid on Britain, then joined Tirpitz for Christmas dinner. But the next day, after the Grossadmiral sent a letter cautioning against anything but an all-out aerial effort, von Pohl repented his decision to act without first gaining the Kaiser's approval and wired Strasser to cancel the attack.[2] The cancellation order was probably academic, for the good weather that Strasser had stressed was being wiped out by the storm that started to arise on the afternoon of the 25th.

This display of indecision provoked a searing letter of criticism from Konteradmiral Philipp, one of the most ardent advocates of aerial bombardment, which apparently goaded von Pohl into taking an action he might have taken much earlier – seeking an audience with the Kaiser under his right of direct access (Immediatvortag) to the emperor to discuss high policy matters. Aerial activity was only one of the items on the agenda for the subsequent meetings, which took place at Charlesville on 8–10 January 1915 and covered the whole spectrum of the naval war, but it was a crucial one. The discussions finally levered the Kaiser into approval of aerial bombing of Britain, although London itself was to be off limits and targets restricted to 'docks and military establishments in the lower Thames and on the English coast.'[3] Von Pohl immediately relayed the decision to fleet headquarters. Finally, the Naval Airship Division was being given a chance to heed the admonition of a song soon to become popular in Germany:

Zeppelin, flieg,	Zeppelin, fly,
Hilf uns im Krieg,	Help us in the war,
Flieg nach England,	Fly to England,
England wird abgebrannt …	England shall be destroyed by fire …

British apprehension about the airships had continued and even increased in the wake of the Cuxhaven Raid. On 1 January, just one week after the attack, Churchill presented the War Council with a memo containing Sueter's estimate that Germany now possessed about 20 airships capable of reaching London, each able to carry a ton of bombs, and stating that the Air Department would be unable to prevent an attack by them once they got into the air.[4] This was a gross exaggeration of airship numbers and load-carrying capacity, but a very accurate appraisal of defence capability. The only answer seemed to be a continuation of the spoiling offensive, and so a repeat of the Cuxhaven Raid, if possible on a larger scale, was looked upon favourably.

Plans for such an operation, again coupled with an attempt to lure the High Seas Fleet to battle, were discussed during early January. Tyrwhitt was eager to stage a repetition of the 28 August surface action, but was frustrated by bad weather. A sweep of the Harwich Force into the bight was scheduled for 15 January, but cancelled the day before by the Admiralty, which summoned the commodore to Whitehall to discuss another air raid. The upshot of his meeting with Churchill and Fisher was a decision to mount an air attack as soon as weather permitted, other operations not requiring seas as favourable, to be continued in the meantime.

But before the opportunity came for the carriers to try again, the long-expected and long-feared finally happened – Zeppelins bombed England.

Strasser had lost no time after receiving the go-ahead. Only the weather deterred the first raid, and that became favourable on 13 January. But the first attempt was a failure after all four North Sea airships – L 5 and L 6 from Nordholz, L 3 and L 4 from Fuhlsbüttel – set out that day. The weather started deteriorating as they flew west along the Frisian chain, and at 1.54pm heavy rain forced them to turn back. Conditions improved again five days later, and on 19 January *L 3*, *L 4* and *L 6* took off again, loaded with high explosive and incendiary bombs, *L 5* being held in reserve for fleet scouting should that be required. Strasser himself was aboard *L 6* but was fated not to reach Britain, for that ship was forced to return when an engine broke down.[6]

L 3 crossed the Norfolk coast at 7.50pm, making an accurate landfall north of Great Yarmouth, a naval base on the German target list. The airship soon found the town and dropped six explosive and seven incendiary bombs on it. *L 4*, bound for the Humber, navigated much less accurately and reached the Norfolk coast, at 8.30pm, far from its target. It scattered bombs on the villages of Sheringham, Thornham, Brancaster, Heachem, Snettisham and King's Lynn. Both airships returned unscathed, landing at Fuhlsbüttel shortly before 8am on 20 January. The first Zeppelin raid on Britain had killed 4 persons and wounded 16, and damaged several houses and a power station.[7] No military objectives had been hit, although the airship commanders thought they had aimed at such targets.

So began, at last, after long months of anticipation on both sides, the airship bombardment of Britain. This campaign was to continue through early 1918, although suffering a severe setback after the autumn of 1916 when effective defensive aerial armament finally came into use. But the January raid was not the start of the onslaught that had been so dreaded. The airships, because of bad weather, lack of numbers, and losses (including the destruction of *L 3* and *L 4* by a storm while on a scouting mission in February), were not able to come again until mid-April, and Greater London was not sanctioned as a target until July.

Ironically, the 19-20 January raid had coincided with Tyrwhitt's long-sought sweep into the bight to attack the German partol lines around Heligoland, and the paths of the airships and the Harwich Force had crossed while both were advancing and retiring, but neither sighted the other. Three days later the weather was judged propitious for the new air raid, and at 1pm on the 23rd* Keyes sailed from Harwich with *Lurcher*, *Firedrake* and eight submarines to carry out a repeat of the Christmas Day performance. But he was quickly recalled, re-entering harbour at 4pm to find the Harwich Force under orders to join Beatty for the interception of an enemy battlecruiser squadron whose activity

---

* The same day that the first of the new airship sheds authorized months earlier at Nordholz finally was completed.

had been discovered by Admiralty electronic intelligence. The result was the Battle of the Dogger Bank the next day. The Harwich Force, reinforced since Christmas by the *Arethusa* class cruiser *Aurora* and seven more 'M' class destroyers, took a prominent part in the clash, *Arethusa* herself rescuing a number of survivors from *Blücher*.

Tyrwhitt's ships had scarcely been tidied up after this action when the seaplane attack that it had cancelled was rescheduled. Emboldened by the immunity from surface attack the Harwich Force had enjoyed on 25 December, the planners of the new operation added a night sweep of the bight, to be carried out by Tyrwhitt's cruisers and destroyers, supported by Beatty's battle-cruisers, after the carriers had collected their aeroplanes and sailed for home. Tyrwhitt postponed a much-needed refit of *Arethusa* so she could take part.

The Harwich Force sailed at 8am on 29 January, but once again the weather became fickle. Within a few hours high north-westerly winds and heavy seas began to affect the carriers so strongly that damage to their planes, only lightly protected by canvas screens, became probable. Even if the seaplanes survived this buffeting, take-off would be impossible should the blow continue. So at 1pm Tyrwhitt ordered a return to port.[8] This ended what turned out to be the final attempt in the entire war to attack the 'Cuxhaven' Zeppelin base by air.

Abandonment of seaborne aerial efforts against the airship base just as the Zeppelin bombing campaign was finally starting seems contradictory. It can only be understood by the realization that it was not a conscious, deliberate policy decision but a product of various factors and circumstances.

Foremost of these was the simple physical obstacle of the North Sea weather, especially during the stormy months. Four times the carriers had actually set sail for the bight, and twice been thwarted by bad weather. Two of the three scheduled raids had to be cancelled for the same reason. The one success in getting planes into the air near the target had met eventual failure because of fog. As long as seaplanes had to be relied upon, this obstacle would remain unchallengable.

Another factor was the loss of the Harwich Force of two-thirds of its carriers. Early in February *Engadine* and *Riviera* were withdrawn from service for refits that amounted almost to reconstruction. This was also attributable to the weather, for the principal reason for their renovation was to give them facilities for safer and more secure carriage of planes, to install more efficient handling and hoisting equipment, and provide improved armament. The experience of 29 January may well have been a factor behind this. For *Engadine* the virtual reconstruction of upper works lasted from 10 February to 24 March, and for *Riviera* from 14 February to 7 April. They emerged with large, slab-sided steel hangars aft, in which seaplanes could shelter secure from wind and wave, plus greatly improved internal arrangements for plane handling and maintenance.

This left the Harwich Force for a time with only *Empress*, whose maximum of three planes was hardly adequate to attempt a raid considering that more than twice that number had been unable to find or attack the Nordholz hangar in December. In February she was detached for a time to assist with bombing raids on the German submarine bases in Belgium.

New aircraft and improved aerial armament appearing in the first months of 1915 enabled a change in anti-airship tactics, for with these the Zeppelin lost at least some of its previous immunity to attack in the air. The aircraft was the Sopwith Schneider, a nimble little single-seater twin-float seaplane whose performance relative to the Zeppelin was much greater than the big two-seater Shorts. The Schneider could be armed with a machine gun, firing upward through a cut-out in the upper wing, and also could carry a special new anti-airship weapon, the Ranken dart. Named after its inventor, Royal Navy Engineer Lieutenant Commander Francis Ranken, this was a slender cylindrical missile containing an explosive charge and having expanding vanes on the tail to grip the fabric of an airship, while the head passed through and detonated. They were housed beneath the plane in a container of 24, and could be released three at a time.

Although these planes and weapons made the prospect of aerial attacks on Zeppelins more feasible than in 1914, the tactic of attacking airships on the ground remained important.

Another factor in the abandonment of attempts to attack Nordholz may have been psychological, although here one is on shaky, undocumented ground. The first Zeppelin attack on England, as so often in human affairs, turned out in reality to be far less terrible than anticipated. Although its damage seemed devastating in an era unfamiliar with the horrors of mass aerial bombing of urban areas, by military standards it was negligible and had been delivered not by the mass squadron of sky monsters so often depicted in prewar days, but by a mere two craft that appeared only briefly. Certainly the raid of 19-20 January took some of the edge off fear of the airship. The craft's real potential as a bomber, however, was yet to be displayed.

But if the aerial menace was somewhat minimized in early 1915, the undersea menace took on an alarming aspect with the German declaration on 4 February of an 'area of war' around the British Isles, tantamount to a blockade and beginning the first period of unrestricted submarine warfare against sea commerce. This much greater threat to Britain's well-being diverted Admiralty attention from the Zeppelin to the U-boat, which was even more difficult to combat than the airship.

A final reason the Cuxhaven Raid was never repeated may be linked to the disappearance of Churchill and Fisher from the Admiralty in late May, both resigning in repercussions from the Dardanelles fiasco. Churchill was replaced as First Lord by Arthur Balfour and Fisher as First Sea Lord by Admiral Sir Harry Jackson. The new regime is generally characterised by naval historians as lack-lustre, prosaic and uninspired in comparison with the Churchill-Fisher combination. Certainly Balfour and Jackson never appreciated the potential of the Royal Naval Air Service to the same extent as their predecessors. One of their first acts was to reorganize the air service,* bringing it more closely under traditional naval discipline and lopping off most of the military appendages it had sprouted under Churchill (although they were to remain responsible for the aerial defence of Britain for many months).

Criticism of the Balfour–Jackson aviation policy has probably been overdone however, for the air service did continue to progress no matter who was sitting on the Board of Admiralty. The anti-aircraft offensive on the Continent went ahead during

---

* One of the victims of this was Sueter, who in September was designated superintendent of aircraft construction for the Air Department and replaced as head of that department by Rear Admiral C L Vaughan-Lee. In early 1917, as the result of his continued advocacy of the torpedo plane, he was sent to command RNAS units in the Adriatic with the idea of undertaking aerial torpedo attacks on the Austro-Hungarian fleet. The only such attempt, however, which was also the only mass aerial torpedo strike tried by the Royal Navy during the war, was unsuccessful. Earlier, Sueter had taken an important part in the development of the tank, and in 1917 indiscreetly wrote directly to King George V seeking some public recognition of that work. This breach of protocol, when it came to attention, damned Sueter forever in the eyes of the Admiralty bureaucracy, which recalled him from his Adriatic command, placed him on half-pay, refused to give him further naval employment and eventually barred his entrance into the new Royal Air Force. Admiralty enmity could not deny him an eventual knighthood and promotion to rear admiral, but it soured him forever on the surface navy. In 1921 he was elected to parliament, where he served for many years as either (depending upon one's viewpoint) a liberal and progressive champion of air power or an embittered crank seeking vengeance against the institution that had blighted his professional career. He died in 1960 at the age of 88.

1915. In June the RNAS pilots at Dunkirk struck at the German army airships that had moved into new bases in Belgium for attacks on London, destroying two Zeppelins (including one bombed in mid-air) and damaging another. This made permanent occupation of the Belgian bases too risky, and from then on they were used by the army's airships only during short periods and by the navy's only in emergencies.[9] The denial of bases so much closer to Britain meant that airship raids had to be mounted from interior Germany, with the Zeppelins having to fly farther and longer and consequently having to carry more fuel to the detriment of bomb loads.

This was the ultimate contribution to British aerial defence from Churchill's policy of distressing the German ships in their havens; it was not a crucial contribution, but it helped.

Although attempts to reach Nordholz were given up, the Harwich Force continued aero-naval operations during the spring of 1915. The first, carried out with only *Empress*, was an attempt to bomb the German radio station at Norddeich on the East Frisian coast and locate a new airship base under construction inland at nearby Hage. It failed because the seaplanes could not take off in 'a lumpy sea and a high wind.'[10] It was tried again three days later, with *Arethusa* and *Aurora* each carrying a seaplane to argument *Empress'* complement. This time fog foiled take-off.

On 20 April *Empress* left to undergo reconstuction of the kind given to *Engadine* and *Riviera*, but at the end of the month was replaced by *Ben-my-Chree*, a former Isle of Man packet converted to a seaplane carrier with the kind of large aft hangar installed on the other carriers. *Engadine* and *Riviera*, their renovation completed, also rejoined, and on 3 May the Harwich Force, with three carriers, four light cruisers and eight destroyers, again tried the Norddeich operation. *Ben-my-Chree* was carrying, probably for the first time in a carrier sortie, a Sopwith Schneider on a forward platform from which it was supposed to take off on trollies under its floats. This raid was frustrated by adverse seas, and a similar attempt on 6 May by fog.

The effort was renewed on 11 May. The engine of *Ben-my-Chree*'s Schneider backfired and could not be started, but *Engadine* got three seaplanes into the air. They were engulfed in fog before they could accomplish anything; one returned safely to the carrier, another crashed and its pilot was lost, the third crashed upon landing because of engine failure but its pilot was saved by a destroyer that salvaged the plane.[11]

After this fiasco it was several months before the Harwich Force made any more attempts to play the aerial 'game'. The carrier squadron was disbanded, although it is not clear whether the failure of 11 May was directly responsible. *Engadine* was sent to Rosyth to become the aviation vessel for Beatty's battlecruisers, and *Riviera* to take a similar role with Admiral Sir Reginald Bacon's Dover Patrol. *Ben-my-Chree*, bearing Malone, Edmonds and Childers, went off to the Aegean, where she replaced *Ark Royal* (whose slow speed made her too vulnerable to German submarines now appearing there) as aviation vessel for the Dardanelles-Gallipoli operation.

In the autumn of 1915 a new carrier was assigned to the Harwich Force. Like *Ben-my-Chree* she was a speedy Isle of Man passenger vessel originally named *Viking* and was renamed *Vindex* after being converted. She was the first of the so-called mixed carriers in the evolution of the flight-deck vessel, equipped with a forward launching platform – larger and more elaborate than *Ben-my-Chree*'s makeshift version – from which landplanes with conventional wheel undercarriages could take off. The first to do so was a Bristol C single-seater biplane 'scout' or fighter, on 3 November. Facilities for handling and launching seaplanes were located aft, as in the earlier carriers. As many as seven aircraft could be crammed into *Vindex*, although space was so limited that the two fighters forward had to be carried disassembled.

November also saw an experiment in flying a wheeled plane from a conventional warship, when on the 5th a French Deperdussin monoplane from the Felixstowe RNAS base took off on a three-track framework erected over *Aurora*'s forecastle. But while the take-off was successful, the launching set-up masked the cruiser's forward 6-inch gun and took 'an appreciable time'[12] to dismantle. Nothing more came of this idea immediately, but later experiments elsewhere finally resulted in development of launching platforms that were fitted to a large number of cruisers before the end of the war.

With the advent of *Vindex*, plans for attacks on the German airship bases were revived. The targets now, however, were to be the Frisian coast base at Hage and another base thought to be at Hoyer in Schleswig, but actually situated at nearby Tondern. Attempts to bomb Hage on 4 December 1915 and 18 and 29 January 1916 were frustrated by the eternal fog and, in the case of the third attempt, a determined German submarine attack that nearly hit *Arethusa*.

The most ambitious effort occurred on 24-25 March 1916 when Tyrwhitt, now flying his broad pendant in cruiser *Cleopatra* after the loss of faithful *Arethusa* to a mine, advanced in daylight to the

Schleswig coast with four other cruisers, *Vindex*, two flotilla leaders, and eight destroyers. This was a far bolder, larger and more complex operation than the Cuxhaven Raid had been, and this time Beatty's battlecruisers were in truly close support, at one time within visual contact. It also nearly resulted in a major action, for the aggressive Admiral Reinhard Scheer, who had taken over command of the High Seas Fleet in January, rose to the lure and advanced his main body into the bight and a day and night of snow squalls and rising seas.

Vindex got five seaplanes away, but engine trouble identical to that suffered on 11 May brought three down in German territory where their crews were captured. Of the two pilots who returned, one bombed what he thought was a factory at Hoyer and the other made the important discovery that the airship base was in fact inland at Tondern. His attempt to attack it, however, failed when the bomb release mechanism jammed.

It was an action-packed day and night for the Harwich Force. Its destroyers sank two German trawlers, and were bombed by enemy seaplanes; one destroyer rammed another that eventually had to be abandoned; *Cleopatra* rammed and sank a German destroyer and then collided with *Undaunted*. Trywhitt and Beatty very nearly came into action with Scheer, and probably would have, had not the German admiral turned his main body back because of heavy seas.[13]

HMS/M *E 11*, the submarine that rescued crews of three seaplanes during the Cuxhaven Raid, seen here returning from a patrol in the Dardanelles and Sea of Marmora in May 1915. She still lacks the deck gun she could have used to destroy the abandoned seaplanes. *US Naval Photographic Center*

This was not the end of British attempts to hit the Zeppelins with an aero-naval combination, but success was not achieved until 19 July 1918. On that day six Sopwith Camel fighters, each carrying two 50-pound bombs, took off from the quasi-flight-deck carrier *Furious* and destroyed Zeppelins *L 54* and *L 60* in the Tondern shed.[14] It was a final vindication of the tactic, but it had taken more than three years of development of aviation vessels and shipboard aircraft to achieve.

No other attempt was ever made after early 1915 to attack the 'Cuxhaven' (ie Nordholz) base, but British naval aircraft did try twice to repeat the reconnaissance flights of 25 December 1914. Both attempts involved the Harwich Force, and a conspicuous part was played in both by a veteran of the 1914 raid, Erskine Childers.*

The reconnaissance was to be preliminary to a bold plan to attack German ships at Schillig Roads with motor torpedo boats (called Coastal Motor Boats, or CMBs). The airmen were to ascertain if there were any protective booms that might bar the CMBs, and to locate German anchorage positions. This was to be done by a flying boat that would proceed directly from Harwich to Tyrwhitt's ships off the German coast, land and refuel from one of the ships, take off for a three- to four-hour reconnaissance, then come down again for another refuelling before returning to base.

The Harwich Force sailed on this mission on 28 September 1916 and the next morning the reconnaissance plane, a Curtiss flying boat,[15] took off from Harwich with a four-man crew including Childers as observer. He was assigned for this mission from the post of intelligence and navigation officer to a motor torpedo boat

* Childers' role in the Irish independence movement and his heroic death have overshadowed his very real contributions to early naval aerial reconnaissance, which have never been adequately appreciated or described by his biographers. He was highly praised for his work in *Ben-my-Chree*, and shortly after his 1916 North Sea flights was promoted to Lieutenant Commander and awarded the Distinguished Flying Cross. In April, 1917, he was sent to the Eastchurch RNAS station to study new techniques in aerial observation but in July was named a secretary of the Irish Convention convoked by Prime Minister David Lloyd George. The convention lasted nine months, after which Childers returned to aerial service. He ended the war as a Major in the Royal Air Force.

One of his post-Armistice duties, before he mustered out in March, 1919, was inspection of the German submarine pens at Bruges in Belgium – massive ferro-concrete structures designed to withstand aerial bombing and a forerunner of those of World War II – and he co-wrote a highly poetic report on their impressive architecture. Childers' subsequent career needs no retelling, but it was ironic that shortly before his execution by firing squad in 1922 this gallant servant of Great Britain was branded by Churchill in a public speech as a 'mischief-making, murderous renegade'. In fairness to Churchill, however, it should be noted that he reversed this judgement seven years later in his book *The Aftermath* and paid tribute to Childers' 'distinction, ability and courage,' citing especially his 'daring and ardour ... in the Cuxhaven Raid.'

squadron, a position he had been holding since his return from the Mediterranean earlier in 1916.

Soon after the take-off, however, Tyrwhitt found that the weather was deteriorating too badly for the flight to proceed. He ordered some of his ships to retrace their course in hopes of signalling to the Curtiss to return to base, while he himself remained at the rendezvous point in case that effort failed. It did, and the Curtiss sighted the Harwich cruisers at 10.15am. Its pilot, Flight Lieutenant A Q Cooper, was ordered by searchlight to return, but could not do so without refuelling. Once down, he found the sea too rough to take off again, and so the plane was taken in tow by destroyer *Landrail* in the hope of finding calmer water after the refuelling. While this operation was taking place a wing of the plane struck the ship's hull and was damaged so badly that flight was now impossible. The destroyer took off the plane's four occupants and towed it nearly all the way back to Harwich before it succumbed to the sea and sank.

The next attempt was made on 22 October. This time *Vindex* was to launch two Short floatplanes and then haul out for home, leaving the aircraft to be recovered by cruisers after the reconnaissance. The observer in one of the Shorts was again Childers. The planes were hoisted out and took off successfully 15 minutes apart, but once again, as in 1914, the German coast was swathed in fog. Nothing could be seen beyond Wangeroog island, although the planes flew as low as 50 feet over the water. Out in the clearer bight two groups of destroyers, totalling 17 ships, were sighted, and Childers took photos of these, of Heligoland and the islands of Langeoog, Baltrum and Norderney. Both planes were recovered successfully by cruisers.[16]

This failure put an end to plans for the CMB raid for nearly a year. When it was finally carried out in August 1918, on a far less ambitious scale, it resulted in disaster for the little boats, five of the six employed being destroyed or disabled by German seaplanes. But while they were being slaughtered, a Sopwith Camel flown from a lighter towed by Harwich Force destroyer *Redoubt* downed Zeppelin *L 53* in flames. It was the war's penultimate less for the Naval Airship Division, appropriately inflicted by the force that had striven so hard for so long to strike at the Zeppelins.

Naval aviation underwent its first period of growth and evolution during World War I. From a force of doubtful reliability and unproved merit, devoid of tactical doctrine and strategic influence, it developed into an essential tool of maritime war, indispensible to the navies of the future. True, the aeroplane had not yet become the ship-killer it would be in World War II, but its potential for that role had been displayed in limited form.

The Royal Navy was foremost in development and use of the air capability, operating more aircraft for more purposes than any other fleet during the entire struggle. A part of that development was the evolution of the flight-deck aircraft carrier, the vessel that would change naval warfare more drastically than it had been changed during half a century – a craft able to project sea power in a radically new dimension over both ocean and land. The first of this new breed of ship became a reality in September, 1918, with the commissioning of HMS *Argus*, a vessel from which succeeding carriers have differed only in increased size and mechanical elaboration. But *Argus* could not have come into being without the pioneering skill, courage and perseverance of men who flew and fought in cruder craft; men whose efforts slowly and at great cost worked out the principles essential to her evolution. And the beginning of that evolutionary struggle can be traced to the chilly, foggy Christmas Day of 1914, when for the first time carrier aircraft went into battle. That is the lasting significance and legacy of the Cuxhaven Raid. There is a great gap in time and distance between the Frisian coast in 1914 and the Falkland Islands in 1982, but it is spanned by that legacy. The Fleet Air Arm men who flew and serviced the carrier-borne jets and helicopters that contributed so crucially to one of Britain's greatest military feats were its direct inheritors.

Epilogue: 1939

Britich warplanes returned to the scene of the Cuxhaven Raid just under a quarter of a century later. The date was 4 September 1939, the first full day of the new German–British conflict. This time the aircraft did not rise from the sea but came from land bases at home – 10 Bristol Blenheims and 14 Vickers Wellingtons of the Royal Air Force, their targets warships in Schillig Roads and the Elbe.

Once again the German coast was veiled in fog. But the fliers found their objectives, the *panzerschiff* (so-called pocket battle-ship) *Admiral Scheer* in Schillig Roads and battleships *Scharnhorst* and *Gnesisenau* at Brunsbüttel. *Admiral Scheer* was taken by surprise by the first flight of five Blenheims, but the two 500-pound bombs that struck her, and others that fell alongside, all failed to explode. She quickly fought back, flaming down five of her attackers. One of them plunged into the bows of light cruiser *Emden*, inflicting the war's first casualties on the German navy. The Wellingtons that attacked at Brunsbüttel achieved nothing; not a single bomb struck its intended target.

The attackers suffered heavily. Seven fell to anti-aircraft fire, so much heavier and more accurate than in 1914, or to fighter planes, which had not existed in 1914.

Thus on the first day of the new war a prized principle of British air power doctrine was literally shot down: the idea that group formations of bombers, by relying on their own defensive gunfire, could function by daylight without fighter escort.[1] The lesson was not learned entirely that first day; for nearly the rest of the year the RAF continued to send unescorted bombers out for armed reconnaissances of the Heligoland Bight or to attack Heligoland island or ships at mainland bases, and nearly always suffered bloody losses. The climax came on 18 December, when a formation of 22 Wellingtons lost 12 planes to fighter attack and 3 that succumbed to battle damage later. After this catastrophe it was a long time before the bombers came again by daylight.

Twenty-five years after the Shorts from *Engadine*, *Riviera* and

Folder No 122, piloted by Flight Commander A B Gaskell was unable to take off and was taken back on board *Engadine*. *By courtesy of P H Liddle via G S Leslie*

Short Type 135, No 136 being hoisted out the water in Kephalo Bay, the Dardanelles in April 1915. *By courtesy of G R Bromet via G S Leslie*

HMS *Lurcher*, the destroyer that was Commodore Roger Keyes' flagship during what he called 'a most memorable Christmas day.' *Imperial War Museum*

Empress had ranged with near-impunity over the north German coast, that coast had become virtually unapproachable to British fliers. What had caused this change? Most of the answers to the question are obvious: vast improvement and expansion of anti-aircraft artillery (*Admiral Scheer* in 1939 mounted more AA guns than the entire High Seas Fleet possessed in 1914); a revolutionary aircraft detection device (radar); and the existence of the fighter plane, a craft unknown in 1914.

But another answer must be that the principles crudely put into practice in the Cuxhaven Raid, then honed and refined during the rest of the war, had long been neglected. The total integration of air and sea craft achieved in 1914 had ceased to exist. For nearly two decades the air service and the sea service had drifted apart, the former taking with it many of the most brilliant men of the latter, including several participants in the Cuxhaven Raid.

Had that rift not occurred, the aerial attacks of 1939 might have been mounted not by high-level bombers spanning the entire North Sea, but by squadrons of the torpedo planes envisioned by Malone and Edmonds, along with dive bombers, both types protected by high-performance fighters,* all three operating from modern versions of the Harwich Force's carriers.

What such a modern 'Cuxhaven Raid' might have accomplished is shown by the results of the Fleet Air Arm attack at Taranto on 11 November 1940. And yet the Taranto attack reveals

---

* It is often argued that only the existence of its independent air force allowed Great Britain to develop the high-performance fighter planes, the Supermarine Spitfire and Hawker Hurricane, that defeated the German aerial assault of 1940; that such craft would not have been created had army and navy retained air arms. Since there is no way to prove or disprove the assertion, its acceptance must be on an *a priori* basis. But the argument ignores the fact that, at first, the Air Ministry actually resisted the new monoplane fighters because they were so much more expensive to build, operate and maintain than the traditional biplanes, and required much larger and costlier ground facilities. If an independent air force were required before the high-performance fighter could be appreciated or acquired, it follows that nations lacking such independent air arms should not have developed such planes. Yet every single one of the fighters employed by the US Army Air Forces in World War II was under design, and some in quantity production, before that service had achieved even quasi-independent status. And total naval control of maritime air branches did not prevent Japan from developing what may have been briefly the finest fighting plane in the world, the Mitsubishi A6M (the so-called Zero), nor the United States from developing carrier fighters eventually superior to the A6M.

the sad state to which British shipboard air power had been reduced by neglect. Taranto was a triumph, but it was also a tragic display of numerical and technical weakness, weakness that enabled the Fleet Air Arm to strike only a temporary crippling blow instead of a permanently annihilating one. The Taranto raid was originally to have been mounted by only 30 carrier aircraft, the most that could be scraped together. The inevitable accidents of war reduced that number to 24 and finally to 21.[2] Thus the attack was carried out by only three times the number of planes the Royal Navy had been able to launch 26 years before, and less than one-tenth of the number the Japanese were to fly over Pearl Harbor 13 months later.

On the technical side, the Taranto raid had to be a night attack because the carrier aircraft involved, the archaic Fairey Swordfish, could not operate in daylight against fighter opposition and the British had no carrier fighters able to counter such opposition. Of the 21 Swordfish, only 12 carried a torpedo, the most important weapon. In contrast, the first Japanese wave at Pearl Harbor included 40 torpedo planes of much higher performance than the Swordfish and carrying much more powerful weapons.

Nothing in the foregoing is intended to denigrate the tactical brilliance of the Taranto operation, the skill, courage and daring of the men who carried it out, or the sagacity of those was planned it. It was marvellous, but it could have been so much more so. It could have completely annihilated the Italian fleet, with all the vast consequences this would have had on the course of the Mediterranean and North African war. But as Nelson remarked, only numbers can annihilate, and the British lacked numbers as well as up-to-date aircraft.

The lack of both can be traced directly to the divergent paths followed by the Royal Navy and Royal Air Force after the creation of the latter in 1918 as a purely political act.[3] Both services can be blamed for the neglect of the seagoing air weapon which soon followed that act, but the rift itself was the cause of the attitudes that led to the neglect. The removal from the navy of a weapon that could and should have been an integral part of its armoury resulted in lack of appreciation, tending to deprecation, of the use of aircraft by the navy. This was simply because, lacking its own aircraft and air personnel, the navy was unable through practice and use to understand the increasing value of aircraft beyond the reconnaissance role. Whether embarked in carrier hangars or on battleship catapults, the aeroplanes belonged to another service. So, equally importantly, did their personnel – save for a small leavening of naval men – and thus could not be fully integrated into naval doctrine and discipline. This failure to appreciate fully the value of aviation at sea caused failure to insist upon and obtain from the Air Ministry the types of aircraft that would eventually be required.

The RAF's faith in air power focused on the bomber, which was seen as the decisive factor in any future conflict. This resulted in the deprecation of naval aircraft as machines useless in the waging of an independent air war. A peculiar situation ensued. The Admiralty did not seek adequate carrier aircraft because the Air Ministry did not develop them, the Air Ministry did not develop them because the Admiralty did not ask for them.[4]

But this is an over-simplification. There were other influential factors at work, among them the shaky state of the British economy and the notorious 'Ten-Year Rule' invoked by politicians year after year to avoid expenditure on any kind of armament.[5] There was also (as air power philosophers have never ceased to remind us *ad nauseam*) a strong element of distrust and dislike of aviation on the part of conservatives in the British naval hierarchy. But to a great extent this was a result rather than a cause of the neglect of aviation. Old-Fogeyism would surely have yielded – at least to the degree it yielded in the American and Japanese navies during the same period – had the former RNAS officers who attained high rank in the air force been able to achieve comparable rank in an aerial arm of their original service.[6]

Whatever the causes, the problem remained the artificial separation of ships and men of the sea from ships and men of the sky. There were those who realized the potential for disaster this separation held, and their arguments against it eventually prevailed. But the Royal Navy did not regain total control of shipboard aviation (and then *only* shipboard aviation, not land- or harbour-based aerial elements) until four months before the start of World War II.* There had been no time to develop and construct, in adequate numbers the aircraft that conflict would require, or to recruit and train the skilled personnel needed to fly and maintain them. And so the Royal Navy went to war in 1939 with an inadequate number of inadequate aeroplanes, just as it had gone to war in 1914 with an inadequate number of inadequate airships. With its main shipboard air strength residing in biplanes that a pilot plucked directly from the cockpit of a Short

---

* Return of the Fleet Air Arm to total naval control was decreed in 1937, the result of the so-called Inskip Award, but a two-year transition period was allowed so that the change-over did not become final until 24 May 1939.

Folder would have found little difficulty in mastering, the navy that had pioneered nearly every aspect of the aircraft carrier had to rely, until later in World War II, on American products to fill its carriers' hangars.

It is the final irony of the Cuxhaven Raid that the principle of aero-naval unification it demonstrated took so long to be rediscovered by the nation that created it.

Notes and References

Chapter 1

1   F Stansbury Haydon, *Aeronautics in the Union and Confederate Armies With a Survey of Military Aeronautics Prior to 1861*, vol 1, (John Hopkins Press, Baltimore 1941), pp 386-97. See also Juliette A Hennessy, 'The Airman's Heritage: Balloons and Airships in the United States Army, 1861-1913', *Aerospace Historian*, vol 16, no 4 (winter 1969) pp 41-7

2   The ascent with Steiner had been suspected for decades as the genesis of Zeppelin's work but documentary proof was not unearthed until the 1960s. See Hans von Schiller, *Zeppelin: Wegbereiter des Weltuftverkehrs* (Kirschbaum Verlag, Bad Godesberg 1967), and Hans von Schiller, 'Count Zeppelin's American balloon ascent (IV)' *Wingfoot Lighter-Than-Air Society Bulletin*, vol 13, no 5 March 1966, p 9

3   For a complete account of Zeppelin's early work and the development of his craft, see von Schiller, *Zeppelin*. Good summaries are given in John B Cuneo, *Winged Mars*, vol 1; *The German Air Weapon 1870-1914*, (Military Service Publishing Co, Harrisburg Pa 1942) and Douglas Robinson, *Giants in the Sky: A History of the Rigid Airship*, (University of Washington Press, Seattle 1973)

4   Quoted in Cuneo, *Winged Mars*, p 53

5   *Ibid*, p 124 and 261

6   For a complete history of the *Mayfly* see Robin Higham, *The British Rigid Airship: A Study in Weapons Policy* (G T Foulis, London 1961)

7   Walter Raleigh and H A Jones, *The War in the Air*, 6 vols, (Oxford University Press, London 1922-37), vol 1, p 181

8   For the complete story, see Higham, *The British Rigid Airship*

9   Winston S Churchill, *The World Crisis*, vol 1, first published 1923, (Charles Scribner's Sons, New York 1951) p 338

10   Robin Higham, 'The Peripheral Weapon in Wartime: A Case Study', in Gerald Jordan (ed), *Naval Warfare in the Twentieth Century 1900-1945: Essays in Honor of Arthur Marder* (Croom Helm and Cran Russak, London and New York 1977), pp 90-104

11   Viscount Hythe (ed), *The Naval Annual 1913* (J Griffin, Portsmouth 1913) p 303. The 1914 edition reduced the number of airships to 27.

12   No history of the German army airship service has yet been produced. For its prewar origins, see Cuneo, *Winged Mars*. A summary of its early wartime operations is contained in John R Cuneo, *The Air Weapon 1914-1916*, vol 2 of *Winged Mars* (Military Service Publishing Co, Harrisburg Pa, 1947)

13   Alfred von Tirpitz, *My Memoirs*, 2 vols, (Dodd Mead, New York 1919), vol 1, p 181

14   From 'The Tirpitz Memorandum of June 1897', quoted in Jonathon Steinberg, *Yesterday's Deterrent: Tirpitz and the Birth of the German Battle Fleet* (Macmillan, New York 1965), p 211

15 For the prewar and early war history of the Naval Airship Division see Douglas Robinson, *The Zeppelin in Combat: A History of the German Naval Airship Division, 1912-1918*, (G T Foulis, London 1962)

16 Ernest Dudley, *Monsters of the Purple Twilight* (George G Harrap, London 1960). The paraphrase is from the famous passage in *Locksley Hall*:

For I dipt into the future, far as human eye could see,
Saw the vision of the world, and all the wonder that would be;
Saw the heavens fill with commerce, argosies of magic sails,
Pilots of the purple twilight ...

Chapter 2

1 For a thorough discussion, see Douglas Robinson, *The Zeppelin in Combat: A History of the German Naval Airship Division, 1912-1918* (G T Foulis, London 1962), pp 48-56

2 *The Illustrated War News*, 21 October 1914, p 40

3 Because of his role in the arguments leading to the so-called Inskip Award of 1937, which restored control of shipboard aircraft to the Royal Navy, Churchill has often been portrayed as a steadfast advocate of the idea that the navy should man and command its own air element. Actually, he wavered on this issue as he did on the airship. For his views in 1914, see 'Extract from Minutes of C.I.D. Sub-Committee on "Allotment and Location of Seaplane and Aeroplane Stations", held on 25 June 1914' (C.I.D. SAS-2, Adm. 1/8621), in S W Roskill (ed), *Documents Relating to the Naval Air Service*, vol 1, 1908-1918 (Navy Record Society, London 1969), pp 148-55. See also a commentary by Roskill in *United States Naval Institute Proceedings*, vol 99, no 8/848 (August 1973), pp 95-6

4 For the early patrols, see Walter Raleigh and H A Jones, *The War in the Air*, vol 1, (Oxford University Press, London) pp 360-61

5 *Ibid*, p 361

6 Winston Churchill, *The World Crisis*, vol 1, first published 1923, p 339

7 *Ibid*, pp 340-45 and Raleigh and Jones, *The War in the Air*, vol 1, pp 374-76

8 Richard Bell Davies, *Sailor in the Air: The Memoirs of Vice-Admiral Bell Davies* (Peter Davies, London 1967), p 104, Davies gives an interesting account of the Eastchurch Squadron's operations from landing at Ostend through the First Battle of Ypres. He became unofficial chief of the squadron's aerial operations while Samson was leading the armoured cars. For the latter's adventures, see Raleigh and Jones, *The War in the Air*, vol 1, and Charles R Samson, *Flights and Fights*, (Benn, London 1930)

9 Interesting as these raids were, a detailed account of them has no place in this study. For details, see Raleigh and Jones, *The War in the Air*, vol 1, and Kenneth Poolman, *Zeppelins Against London*, (John Day, New York 1961)

10 At least this seems to have been the reason. See Robinson, *The Zeppelin in Combat*, p 43

Chapter 3

1 Graham Wallace, *Claude Grahame-White: A Biography* (Putnam, London 1967), p 196. I have found no other souce confirming this proposal.

2 Walter Raleigh and H A Jones, *The War in the Air*, vol 1, (Oxford University Press, London), p 368

3 Complete particulars of these vessel can be found in various volumes listed in the bibliography
4 There is some disagreement on the exact speed of these vessels, but the consensus is that *Engadine* and *Riviera* could do at least 21 knots and *Empress* at least 18 knots. *Engadine* apparently was capable of even faster short spurts. An American destroyer officer reported seeing her make 25 knots in April 1918. More than two decades later as SS *Corregidor* in the Philippines, where she was lost to a mine in December, 1941, she reportedly could do 22 knots after turbine overhauls. See Lt Cdr George Pollak, 'From Dover Straits to Corregidor Deep', *United States Naval Institute Proceedings* 79, no 2 (February 1952), p 149 and Vaughan C Chambers in 'Discussions, Comments, Notes', *USNIP* 79, no 7 (July 1952), p 783
5 His absence may be linked to a puzzling and inaccurate statement 14 years later than 'In December, 1914, I obtained from Mr Churchill permission to send some seaplanes into the Heligoland Bight, to ascertain the whereabouts of the German Fleet, and also to drop bombs on points of military importance', Murray F Sueter, *Airmen or Noahs: Fair Play for Our Airmen* (Sir Isaac Pitman & Sons, London 1928), p 9. In this one sentence Sueter sweeps aside the earlier attempts to mount the raid, gives himself sole credit for the raid as finally carried out, and ignores, in contradiction to his own orders in 1914, the fact that the airship base was the prime target of the operation.
6 Julian S Corbett and Henry Newbolt, *Naval Operations*, 5 vols (Longmans, Green & Co. London 1920-31), vol 1, p 238
7 Quoted in A Temple Patterson, *Tyrwhitt of the Harwich Force: The Life of Admiral of the Fleet Sir Reginald Tyrwhitt* (Macdonald, London 1973), p 82
8 'Minute by Mr Churchill to Director, Air Department, dated 26 October 1914 on "Launching Aircraft from Barges". Papers of Group Captain H A Williamson R.A.F.', in S W Roskill (ed), *Documents Relating to the Naval Air Service*, vol 1, *1908-1918* (Navy Records Society, London 1969), pp 183-4
9 Roskill's comment, *ibid*, p 183
10 See Arthur J Marder, *From the Dreadnought to Scapa Flow: The Royal Navy in the Fisher Era, 1904-1919*, 5 vols (Oxford University Press, London 1961-70), vol 2, pp 85-9
11 Quoted in Churchill, *The World Crisis*, vol 1, (Charles Scribner's Sons, New York 1951), p 489
12 Quoted, *ibid*
13 Quoted, *ibid*, pp 489-90
14 Viscount Jellicoe of Scapa, *The Grand Fleet 1914-1916: Its Creation, Development and Work* (George H Doran, New York 1919), p 164
15 Winston S Churchill, *World Crisis*, vol 1, p 490
16 Quoted in Patterson, *Tyrwhitt of the Harwich Force*, p 89. The reference to anti-aircraft guns in the plural indicates *Arethusa* may have been armed with more than the one 6-pounder high-angle gun usually credited to her in 1914
17 Jellicoe, *The Grand Fleet*, p 164
18 Quoted in Patterson, *Tyrwhitt of the Harwich Force*, p 89
19 H W Wilson, *Battleships in Action*, 2 vols, (Sampson, Low, Marston & Co, London 1926), vol 2, p 84
20 William Jameson, *The Fleet That Jack Built: Nine Men Who Made a Modern Navy* (Harcourt, Brace & World, New York 1962), p 260

Chapter 4

Note: In this chapter and those following I have made use of Air 1/2099, Public Record Office, entitled 'Seaplane Operations Against Cuxhaven Carried Out on

25th December 1914.'. Although printed and bound as one document, it is composed of two documents, numbered 207/20/4 and 207/22/4. There are 10 parts, entitled: Orders of Director of Air Department, Orders Issued by Commodore (T), Orders Issued by Commodore (S), Orders Issued by Commanding Officer of Seaplane Carriers, First Report by Commodore (T), Second Report by Commodore (T), Report by Commodore (S), Report by HMS *Engadine*, Report by HMS *Riviera* and Report by HMS *Empress*. The carrier reports include a summary by each vessel's commanding officer followed by individual reports from pilots who flew from the vessel. Appended to Tyrwhitt's second report is the text of a German radio message describing the raid. Appended to the whole is a Summary of Seaplane Operations plus two extracts from non-RNAS sources.

In these and subsequent notes Air 1/2099 is cited as Seaplane Operations, followed by a reference to the part quoted.

1 A Temple Patterson, *Tyrwhitt of the Harwich Force: The Life of Admiral of the Fleet Sir Reginald Tyrwhitt* (Macdonald, London 1973), p 94
2 Roger Keyes, *The Naval Memoirs of Admiral of the Fleet Sir Roger Keyes*, 2 vols (Thornton Butterworth, London 1934-35), vol 1, p 153
3 Seaplane Operations; Sueter's orders
4 *Ibid*
5 For complete technical details of the three types of seaplane, as far as they have survived, see J M Bruce, *British Aeroplanes 1914-1918* (Putnam, London 1957)
6 Keyes, *Memoirs*, vol 1, p 158
7 Burke Wilkinson, *The Zeal of the Convert* (Robert B Luce, Washington and New York 1976), p 125
8 Seaplane Operations; *Engadine* report
9 Seaplane Operations; *Riviera* report. Emphasis in the original
10 Keyes, *Memoirs*, vol 1, p 158
11 Walter Raleigh and H A Jones, *The War in the Air*, vol 2, pp 156-7
12 Seaplane Operations; Malone's orders
13 *Ibid*
14 Seaplane Operations; Keyes' orders
15 *Ibid*
16 Seaplane Operations; Tyrwhitt's orders
17 *Ibid*
18 *Ibid*
19 *Ibid*
20 *Ibid*
21 Cost figures for the 1914 seaplanes are not known, but later in the war the standard production model Short 184 seaplane cost £3107. 10s for airframe minus engine, instruments and armament, while its engine cost £1391.10s (Bruce, *British Aeroplanes*, p 495). It can be assumed that the engines of the 1914 craft represented one-fourth to one-third of the planes' entire monetary value.
22 Seaplane Operations; Tyrwhitt's orders
23 See Keyes, *Memoirs*, vol 1, p 155
24 Patterson, *Tyrwhitt of the Harwich Force*, p 95; Wilkinson, *The Zeal of the Convert*, pp 133-4

Chapter 5

1 For a detailed description of the Grand Fleet's movements this day, see Viscount Jellicoe of Scapa, *The Grand Fleet 1914-1916: Its Creation, Development and Work* (George H Doran, New York 1919), pp 182-3

2   Seaplane Operations; *Engadine* report (see notes to chapter 4 for explanation of this citation).

3   Seaplane Operations; *Riviera* report

4   For a description, see Neville Jones, *The Origins of Strategic Bombing: A Study of the Development of British Air Strategic Thought and Practice up to 1918* (William Kimber, London 1973), pp 70-1

5   Bryan Cooper and John Batchlor, *Bombers 1914-1939* (Phoebus, London nd), pp 26-7

6   Seaplane Operations; Malone's report

7   *Ibid*, Gaskell Blackburn's report in *Empress* report

8   John A de Vries, *Taube, Dove of War* (Historical Aviation Album, Temple City, California 1978), p 12. See also Walter Raleigh and H A Jones, *The War in the Air*, vol 3, (Oxford University Press, London 1922–37), p 89

9   Seaplane Operations; Tyrwhitt's first report. In this report Tyrwhitt gives the time of sighting of the supposed German vessels as 4.30am. However, in a quotation in William Jameson, *The Fleet That Jack Built: Nine Men Who Made a Modern Navy* (Harcourt, Brace & World, New York 1962), p 260, he gives it as 4am. The quotation, from a letter to his sister written several days after the operation, indicates Tyrwhitt was misremembering times, for he also states in it that at 4am his ships were still three hours steaming from the seaplane launching position. In fact, at that time the ships were two hours distant, for in their reports both the commodore and Malone state the take-off point was reached at 6am.

10   Quoted in Jameson, *The Fleet That Jack Built*, p 260

11   The *S 1* was the first of a class of three boats built to an Italian design, displacing 255 tons surface, 390 tons submerged (some sources give 252 tons surface, 386 tons submerged or 265 tons surface and 386 tons submerged). She was thus no more than half the size of the 'D' and 'E' classes with correspondingly lesser range and endurance, and it can be surmised that for this reason she was assigned the westermost station during the Cuxhaven operation. The design proved unsatisfactory in service and all three 'S' class boats were turned over to Italy in 1915, the last before she ever commissioned in the Royal Navy.

12   Keyes, *The Naval Memoirs of Admiral of the Fleet Sir Roger Keyes*, 2 vols (Thornton Butterworth, London 1934-35), vol 1, p 158

13   Quoted in Jameson, *The Fleet That Jack Built*, p 260. A slightly different version of the story is given in Patterson, *Tyrwhitt of the Harwich Force: The Life of Admiral of the Fleet Sir Reginald Tyrwhitt* (Macdonald, London 1973), pp 95-6

14   Quoted in Jameson, *The Fleet That Jack Built*, p 260

15   Seaplane Operations; *Engadine* report

16   *Ibid*, *Empress* report

17   *Ibid*, *Engadine* report

18   *Ibid*, Tyrwhitt's first report

19   *Ibid*, *Engadine* report

20   The problem of 'unsticking' in calm water, as noted earlier, was to plague naval seaplanes for decades. As late as November 1942, American seaplanes far more powerful than the Shorts of 1914 spent more than an hour trying to lift off from becalmed Tulagi harbour to take part in the Battle of Tassafaronga. See Samuel Eliot Morison, *History of United States Naval Operations in World War II*, vol 5, *The Struggle for Guadalcanal: August 1942–February 1943* (Little, Brown, Boston 1958), p 299

Chapter 6

1 Daniel Horn, (ed and trans), *The Private War of Seaman Stumpf: The Unique Diaries of a Young German in the Great War* (Leslie Frewin, London 1969) p 58
2 Reinhard Scheer, *Germany's High Sea Fleet in the World War* (Cassell, London and New York 1920), p 11. See also Arthur J Marder, *From the Dreadnought to Scapa Flow: The Royal Navy in the Fisher Era, 1904-1919*, 5 vols (Oxford University Press, London and New York 1961-70), vol 2, pp 42-5
3 Scheer, *Germany's High Sea Fleet*, chapter 3
4 *Ibid*, p 30
5 *Ibid*
6 Actually, a few inches larger in all three dimensions
7 Douglas Robinson, *The Zeppelin in Combat: A History of the German Naval Airship Division, 1912-1918* (G T Foulis, London 1962), p 45
8 Otto Groos and Walther Gladisch, *Der Krieg in der Nordsee*, 7 vols, (Mittler, Berlin 1920-65) vol 3, p 129
9 Quoted in Robinson, *The Zeppelin in Combat*, p 42
10 John R Cuneo, *The Air Weapon 1914-1916* (Military Service Publishing Co, Harrisburg Pa 1947), p 301
11 Julian Corbett and Henry Newbolt, *Naval Operations*, 5 vols, (Longmans, Green & Co, London 1920-31), vol 1, p 212
12 Winston S Churchill, *The World Crisis*, vol 1, p 500
13 Scheer, *Germany's High Sea Fleet*, p 75
14 Groos and Gladisch, *Krieg in Nordsee*, vol 3, p 127
15 *Ibid*, vol 3, pp 126-7
16 Cuneo, *Air Weapon*, p 303
17 Groos and Gladisch, *Krieg in Nordsee*, vol 3, p 127
18 Horn, *The Private War of Seaman Stumpf*, p 25
19 *Ibid*, p 46
20 Groos and Gladisch, *Krieg in Nordsee*, vol 3, p 127
21 *Ibid*
22 *Ibid*
23 *Ibid*, vol 3, pp 128-9
24 *Ibid*, vol 3, p 127. Emphasis in the original. This passage, which is not a quotation from the *U 6* sighting report but was written by Groos, is open to question, smacking of insertion of information gained ex post facto. Groos' third volume on the North Sea naval war appeared two years after publication of vol 2 of Corbett's *Naval Operations*, which covers the Cuxhaven Raid and which Groos drew upon for his descriptions of British strength and movements on 25 December. It is reasonable to expect that a submarine commander could identify British cruisers and destroyers by class; what is singularly suspicious about the passage is the mention of 'large superstructures at the stern' of the carriers. The large after-deck hangars that were later conspicuous recognition features of these ships were not installed until their remodelling in early 1915. In December there was little to distinguish the carriers at a distance from any small passenger vessels.
25 *Ibid*, vol 3, p 128
26 *Ibid*, vol 3, pp 127-8
27 See note 24
28 Groos and Gladisch, *Krieg in Nordsee*, vol 3, p 128

Chapter 7

1   Douglas Robinson, *The Zeppelin in Combat: A History of the German Naval Airship Division, 1912-1918* (G T Foulis, London 1962), p 46
2   From Ross, Kilner–Childers and Miley reports, respectively, in Seaplane Operations (see notes to chapter 4 for explanation of this citation)
3   Seaplane Operations; Hewlett's report in *Riviera* report
4   *Ibid*
5   *Ibid*
6   *Ibid*
7   *Ibid*
8   Seaplane Operations; Ross's report in *Engadine* report
9   *Ibid*
10   *Ibid*
11   *Ibid*
12   *Ibid*
13   Seaplane Operations; Miley's report in *Engadine* report
14   *Ibid*
15   Seaplane Operations; Oliver's report in *Empress* report
16   *Ibid*
17   Seaplane Operations; Edmonds' report in *Riviera* report
18   *Ibid*
19   Otto Groos and Walther Gladisch, *Der Krieg in der Nordsee*, 7 vols, (Mittler, Berlin 1920-65), vol 3 p 129
20   *Ibid*
21   Seaplane Operations; Gaskell Blackburn's report in *Empress* report
22   *Ibid*
23   *Ibid*
24   *Ibid*
25   *Ibid*
26   Robert Jackson, *Strike From the Sea: A Survey of British Naval Air Operations, 1909-1969* (Arthur Barker, London 1970), p 24
27   Seaplane Operations; Gaskell Blackburn's report in *Empress* report
28   *Ibid*
29   *Ibid*
30   Seaplane Operations; Kilner-Childers report in *Riviera* report
31   *Ibid*
32   *Ibid*
33   *Ibid*
34   *Ibid* This is the only mention in Seaplane Operations of the supposed existence of such a base, which does not appear in the Admiralty list of reconnaissance objectives. There is no explanation of why Childers apparently thought such a facility might exist on Wangeroog.
35   Groos and Gladisch, *Krieg in Nordsee*, vol 3, p 130
36   *Ibid*, vol 3, p 129. See also Robinson, *The Zeppelin in Combat*, p 43
37   Seaplane Operations; Malone's orders

Chapter 8

1 Otto Groos and Walther Gladisch, *Der Krieg in der Nordsee*, 7 vols, (Mittler, Berlin 1920-65), vol 3 p 128

2 A Temple Patterson, *Tyrwhitt of the Harwich Force: The Life of Admiral of the Fleet Sir Reginald Tyrwhitt* (Macdonald, London 1973), p 97

3 Seaplane Operations; *Empress* report (see notes to chapter 4 for explanation of this citation)

4 Groos and Gladisch, *Krieg in Nordsee*, vol 3, p 130

5 *Ibid*

6 Quoted in Douglas Robertson, *The Zeppelin in Combat: A History of the German Naval Airship Division, 1912-1918* (G T Foulis, London 1962), p 45

7 Seaplane Operations; Tyrwhitt's first report

8 *Ibid*; *Empress* report

9 Groos and Gladisch, *Krieg in Nordsee*, vol 3 p 133

10 Seaplane Operations; *Empress* report

11 *Ibid*

12 *Ibid*

13 *Ibid*; Tyrwhitt's second report

14 Groos and Gladisch, *Krieg in Nordsee*, vol 3, p 130

15 The holes numbered three, according to Groos and Gladisch, *Krieg in Nordsee*, vol 3, p 131; nine, according to Robinson, *The Zeppelin in Combat*, p 46

16 Roger Keyes, *The Naval Memoirs of Admiral of the Fleet Sir Roger Keyes*, 2 vols, (Thornton Butterworth, London 1933-35), vol 1, p 154

17 Seaplane Operations; Tyrwhitt's first report

18 *Ibid*, Tyrwhitt's second report

19 Groos and Gladsich, *Krieg in Nordsee*, vol 3, pp 132-3

20 Seaplane Operations; Tyrwhitt's second report

21 Statement of an unidentified German naval officer given in C F Snowden Gamble, *The Story of a North Sea Air Station* (Oxford University Press, London 1928), p 115. See also Arthur Hezlet, *Aircraft and Sea Power* (Stein and Day, New York 1970), pp 29-30

22 Seaplane Operations; Gaskell Blackburn's report in *Empress* report

23 *Ibid*; Oliver's report in *Empress* report

24 Groos and Gladisch, *Krieg in Nordsee*, vol 3, p 132

25 *Ibid*, vol 3, p 131

26 *Ibid*, vol 3, p 133

27 *Ibid*

28 Seaplane Operations; Tyrwhitt's second report

29 Groos and Gladisch, *Krieg in Nordsee*, vol 3, p 143

30 This account of the German submarine activity is condensed from that given in Groos, *Krieg in Nordsee*, vol 3, pp 135-8. Some reports of sightings of British submarines have been omitted

31 Seaplane Operations; Tyrwhitt's first report

32 *Ibid*, Keyes' report

33 *Ibid* Tyrwhitt's first report

34 Groos and Gladisch, *Krieg in Nordsee*, vol 3, p 139

35 Gamble, *North Sea Air Station*, p 114. The same quoted source as in note no 21 above. There were lower deck rumours in the High Seas Fleet that two British seaplanes had been recovered. The origin of the 'Avro' identification may reside in the fact that the Imperial Navy had a few Avro floatplanes

among the foreign types in its prewar inventory. One of these made the first aeroplane flight to Heligoland from the mainland

36 Seaplane Operations; Keyes' report
37 *Ibid; Riviera* report
38 Keyes, *Memoirs*, vol 1, p 154
39 Seaplane Operations; Keyes' report
40 Keyes, *Memoirs*, vol 1, p 157
41 *Ibid*
42 Groos and Gladisch, *Krieg in Nordsee*, vol 3, p 138
43 Keyes, *Memoirs*, vol 1, p 157
44 Seaplane Operations; Hewlett's report in *Riviera* report
45 John Leyland, (ed), Brassey's *Naval Annual* 1915 (William Clowes, London 1915), p 71
46 Seaplane Operations; Hewlett's report in *Riviera* report
47 Viscount Jellicoe of Scapa, *The Grand Fleet 1914–1916: Its Creation, Development and Work* (George H Doran, New York 1919), p 183
48 Robinson, *The Zeppelin in Combat*, pp 46-7

Chapter 9

1 Seaplane Operations; *Engadine* report. (See notes to chapter 4 for explanation of this citation.)
2 'The Air Raid on Cuxhaven', *Navy and Army* 2 (new series), no 21, 9 January 1915, pp 370-1
3 Seaplane Operations; 'Extract from Naval Notes dated 27.1.1915', appendix to Summary of Seaplane Operations.
4 *Ibid*
5 Daniel Horn, (ed and trans), *The Private War of Seaman Stumpf: The Unique Diaries of a Young German in the Great War* (Leslie Frewin, London 1969), p 58
6 Murray F Sueter, *Airmen or Noahs: Fair Play for Our Airmen* (Sir Isaac Pitman & Sons, London 1928), p 10
7 Julian Corbett and Henry Newbolt, *Naval Operations*, 5 vols (Longmans, Green & Co, London 1920-31), vol 2, p 51
8 Walter Raleigh and H A Jones, *The War in the Air*, vol 1, p 405
9 Seaplane Operations; 'Copy of the Norddeich W T Message on Plan Y', appendix to Tyrwhitt's second report
10 Corbett and Newbolt, *Naval Operations*, vol 2, pp 52-3 and 84
11 Roger Keyes, *The Naval Memoirs of Admiral of the Fleet Sir Roger Keyes*, 2 vols (Thornton Butterworth, London 1933-5), vol 1, p 157
12 Otto Groos and Walther Gladisch, *Der Krieg in der Nordsee*, 7 vols (Mittler, Berlin 1920-65), vol 3, p 130
13 Seaplane Operations; 'Extracts from M01052', appendix to Summary of Seaplane Operations
14 Paul Schmalenbach, 'SMS Blücher', *Warship International* 8, no 2, (1971) pp 171-81. Additional information supplied to the author by Paul Schmalenbach
15 Corbett and Newbolt, *Naval Operations*, vol 2, p 82; Groos and Gladisch, *Krieg in Nordsee*, vol 3, p 140

16   Douglas Robinson, *The Zeppelin in Combat: A History of the German Naval Airship Division, 1912-1918* (G T Foulis, London 1962), p 46
17   Seaplane Operations; *Empress* report
18   *Ibid*
19   Seaplane Operations; Tyrwhitt's first report
20   Seaplane Operations; *Empress* report
21   Seaplane Operations; Tyrwhitt's second report
22   *Ibid*
23   Seaplane Operations; *Riviera* report
24   Seaplane Operations; *Engadine* report
25   Sueter memorandum of 20 December 1916, Adm. 1/8477, Public Record Office, in S W Roskill (ed), *Documents Relating to the Naval Air Service*, vol 1, *1908-1918* (Navy Records Society, London 1969), p 436
26   Seaplane Operations; *Engadine* report
27   Groos and Gladisch, *Krieg in Nordsee*, vol 3, pp 134-5 and 138
28   *Ibid*, vol 3, p 135
29   *Ibid*, vol 3, p 134
30   *Ibid*
31   Seaplane Operations; Tyrwhitt's first report
32   Quoted in A Temple Patterson, *Tyrwhitt of the Harwich Force: The Life of Admiral of the Fleet Sir Reginald Tyrwhitt* (Macdonald, London 1973), p 98
33   Quoted in Sueter, *Airmen or Noahs*, p 11

Chapter 10

1   Walter Gorlitz, (ed), Mervyn Savill, (trans), *The Kaiser and His Court: The Diaries, Note Books and Letters of Admiral Georg Alexander von Müller, Chief of the Naval Cabinet, 1914-1918* (Harcourt, Bruce & World, New York 1964), p 51
2   Douglas Robinson, *The Zeppelin in Combat: A History of the German Naval Airship Division, 1912-1918* (G T Foulis, London 1962), pp 54-5
3   Quoted in Robinson, *The Zeppelin in Combat*, p 56. For the Charleville conference, see *idem*, pp 55-6, and Gorlitz, *The Kaiser and His Court*, pp 53-5
4   Churchill memorandum, Cab. 37/123, Public Record Office, in S W Roskill, (ed), *Documents Relating to the Naval Air Service*, vol 1, *1908-1918* (Navy Records Society, London 1969), pp 188-9
5   A Temple Patterson, *Tyrwhitt of the Harwich Force: The Life of the Admiral of the Fleet Sir Reginald Tyrwhitt* (Macdonald, London 1973), p 99
6   Robinson, *The Zeppelin in Combat*, pp 57-8
7   *Ibid*, pp 58-65; Walter Raleigh and H A Jones, *The War in the Air*, 6 vols (Oxford University Press, London 1922-37), vol 3, pp 90-1
8   Patterson, *Tyrwhitt of the Harwich Force*, p 112. The abortive attempts of 23 and 29 January are not mentioned in the British official air and naval histories.
9   Robinson, *The Zeppelin in Combat*, p 77
10   Walter Raleigh and H A Jones, *The War in the Air*, vol 2, p 358
11   *Ibid*, vol 2, p 359; Ian M Burns, 'Woman of My Heart: The Story of HMS *Ben-my-Chree*', part 1, *Cross & Cockade (Great Britain) Journal* 6, no 4 (winter 1975), pp 145-57
12   Walter Raleigh and H A Jones, *The War in the Air*, vol 4, p 24. See also J M Bruce, 'Carrier Operations – the Pioneers', *Aircraft Illustrated Extra* 12, nd, pp 4-11

13   For details of this operation, see Walter Raleigh and H A Jones, *The War in the Air*, vol 2, pp 396-401; Patterson, *Tyrwhitt of the Harwich Force*, pp 152-5; Julian Corbett and Henry Newbolt, *Naval Operations*, 5 vols (Longmans, Green & Co., London 1920-31), vol 3, pp 290-6

14   See R D Layman, 'Furious and the Tondern Raid', *Warship International* 10, no 4, (1973) pp 374-85

15   This craft is identified only as an America flying boat in Raleigh and Jones, *The War in the Air*, vol 2, p 420, but it was probably a Curtiss H 4 'Small America', retroactively named after the introduction of the H 12 'Large America'.

16   For the reconnaissance attempts of September and October, see Walter Raleigh and H A Jones, *The War in the Air*, vol 2, pp 420-2, and Patterson, *Tyrwhitt of the Harwich Force*, pp 173-4. Patterson states Childers and his pilot landed on the bight for a time to discuss procedures, but the official history identifies the other Short as the one that landed.

Epilogue

1   Philip Joubert de la Ferté, *The Third Service: The Story Behind the Royal Air Force* (Thames and Hudson, London 1955), pp 128-9

2   B B Schofield, *The Attack on Taranto* (Naval Institute Press, Annapolis 1973), pp 26-8

3   See Paul C Phillips, 'Decision and Dissention – Birth of the RAF', *Aerospace Historian* 12, no 1, (1971), pp 33-9

4   The interwar conflict between Admiralty and Air Ministry over air policy is the subject of a large body of writing. For one of the best discussions, see Stephen Roskill, *Naval Policy Between the Wars*, vol 1, *The Period of Anglo-American Antagonism, 1919-1929* (Walker and Co, New York 1968), chapters 6, 10, 13 and 15

5   For a detailed and excellent analysis of the factors affecting and limiting British naval air strength, see Geoffrey Till, *Air Power and the Royal Navy 1914-1945; A Historical Survey* (Jane's Publishing Co, London 1979), especially chapter 8

6   A view that has been speculated upon by British naval historian Stephen Roskill. See his *Churchill and the Admirals* (William Morrow, London 1978), p 71

Bibliography

The works listed below are additional and supplementary to those mentioned in chapter notes and references.

BLUME, AUGUST G 'German Naval Air Service', unpublished manuscript

BONE, REGINALD JOHN 'A Record of Good Luck', *Cross & Cockade (Great Britain) Journal* 9, no 1, 1978

BREMBACH, HELLMUTH *Adler über See: Fünfzig Jahre deutsche Marineflieger*, (Gerhard Stalling, Oldenburg and Hamburg 1962)

CHALMERS, W S *The Life and Letters of David, Earl Beatty*, (Hodder and Stoughton, London 1951)

CHILDERS, ERSKINE *The Riddle of the Sands: A Record of Secret Service*, 1903; (reprinted Penguin Books, Middlesex 1955)

COLLEDGE, J J *Ships of the Royal Navy: An Historical Index*, vol 2, (David & Charles, Newton Abbot 1970)

DITTMAR, F J and COLLEDGE, J J *British Warships 1914-1919*, (Ian Allan, London 1972)

EDWARDS, KENNETH *We Dive at Dawn*, (Reilly & Lee, Chicago 1941)

GIBSON, LANGHORNE, and HARPER, J E T *The Riddle of Jutland: An Authentic History*, (Coward-McCann, New York 1934)

GOODALL, MICHAEL H 'F E T Hewlett and the Cuxhaven Raid', *Cross & Cockade (Great Britain) Journal* 6, no 2, 1975

GRAY, EDWYN *The Undersea War: Submarines 1914-1918*, (Charles Scribner's Sons, New York 1971)

GRAY, PETER and THETFORD, OWEN *German Aircraft of the First World War*, (Putnam, London 1962)

GRÖNER, ERICH *Die deutschen Kriegsschiffe 1815-1945*, (2 vols, J F Lehmanns, Munich 1966-8)

HÜMMELCHEN, GERHARD *Die Deutschen Seeflieger 1935-1945*, (J F Lehmanns, Munich 1976)

HURREN, B J *Perchance: A Short History of British Naval Aviation*, (Nicholson & Watson, London 1949)

KEMP, P K *Fleet Air Arm* (Herbert Jenkins, London 1954)

KILLEN, JOHN *A History of Marine Aviation 1911-68*, (Frederick Muller, London 1969)

LE FLEMING, H M *Warships of World War I*, combined edn, (Ian Allan, London nd)

LIPSCOMB, F W *The British Submarine*, 2nd edn, (Conway Maritime Press, Greenwich 1975)

MACINTYRE, DONALD *Wings of Neptune: The Story of Naval Aviation*, (W W Norton, New York 1964)

MACINTYRE, DONALD *Aircraft Carrier: The Majestic Weapon*, (Ballantine Books, New York 1968)

MCINERNEY, MICHAEL *The Riddle of Erskine Childers*, (E & T O'Brian, Dublin 1971)

MOORE, R 'HMS Engadine', *Model Maker & Model Boats* 16, no 191, (November 1966)

NOWARRA, HEINZ J; ROBERTSON, BRUCE and COOKSELY, PETER G *Marine Aircraft of the 1914-1918 War*, (Harleyford, Letchworth 1966)

POPHAM, HUGH *Into Wind: A History of British Naval Flying*, (Hamish Hamilton, London 1969)

SCRIVENER, W 'Aircraft Carrier Careers', *Warships Supplement* 3, (World Ship Society, June 1966)

SKELTON, MARVIN L 'Gordon S Shephard – A Name Remembered', *Cross & Cockade (Great Britain) Journal* 8, no 1, (1975)

TAYLOR, JOHN C *German Warships of World War I*, (Doubleday, New York 1970)

THETFORD, OWEN *British Naval Aircraft 1912-58* (Putnam, London 1958)

Index

Note: Numerals in italic refer to photographs and their captions.